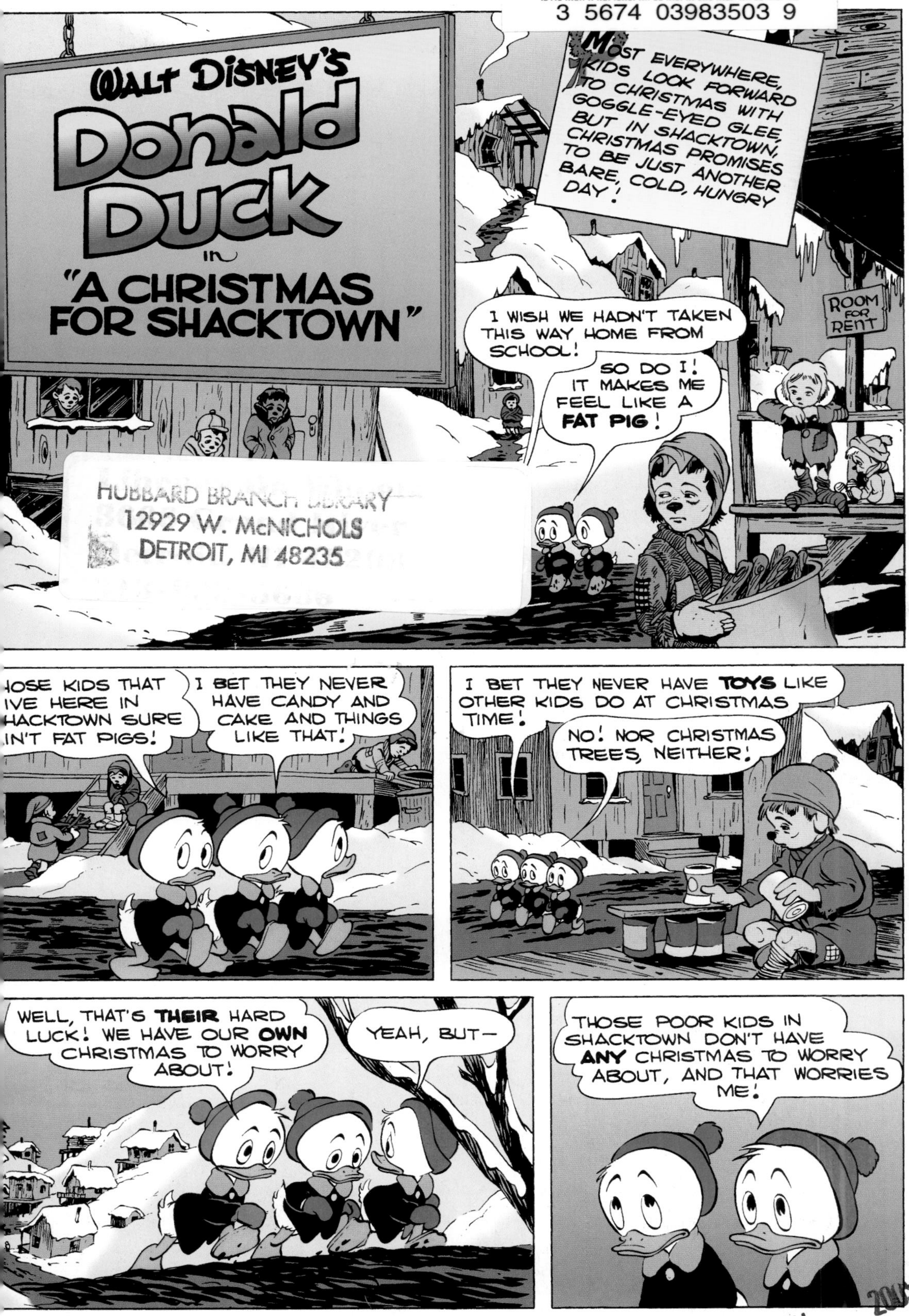
WALT DISNEY'S
Donald Duck
in
"A CHRISTMAS FOR SHACKTOWN"
MOST EVERYWHERE, KIDS LOOK FORWARD TO CHRISTMAS WITH GOGGLE-EYED GLEE, BUT IN SHACKTOWN, CHRISTMAS PROMISES TO BE JUST ANOTHER BARE, COLD, HUNGRY DAY!
ROOM FOR RENT
I WISH WE HADN'T TAKEN THIS WAY HOME FROM SCHOOL!
SO DO I! IT MAKES ME FEEL LIKE A **FAT PIG**!
HOSE KIDS THAT IVE HERE IN HACKTOWN SURE IN'T FAT PIGS!
I BET THEY NEVER HAVE CANDY AND CAKE AND THINGS LIKE THAT!
I BET THEY NEVER HAVE **TOYS** LIKE OTHER KIDS DO AT CHRISTMAS TIME!
NO! NOR CHRISTMAS TREES, NEITHER!
WELL, THAT'S **THEIR** HARD LUCK! WE HAVE OUR **OWN** CHRISTMAS TO WORRY ABOUT!
YEAH, BUT—
THOSE POOR KIDS IN SHACKTOWN DON'T HAVE **ANY** CHRISTMAS TO WORRY ABOUT, AND THAT WORRIES ME!

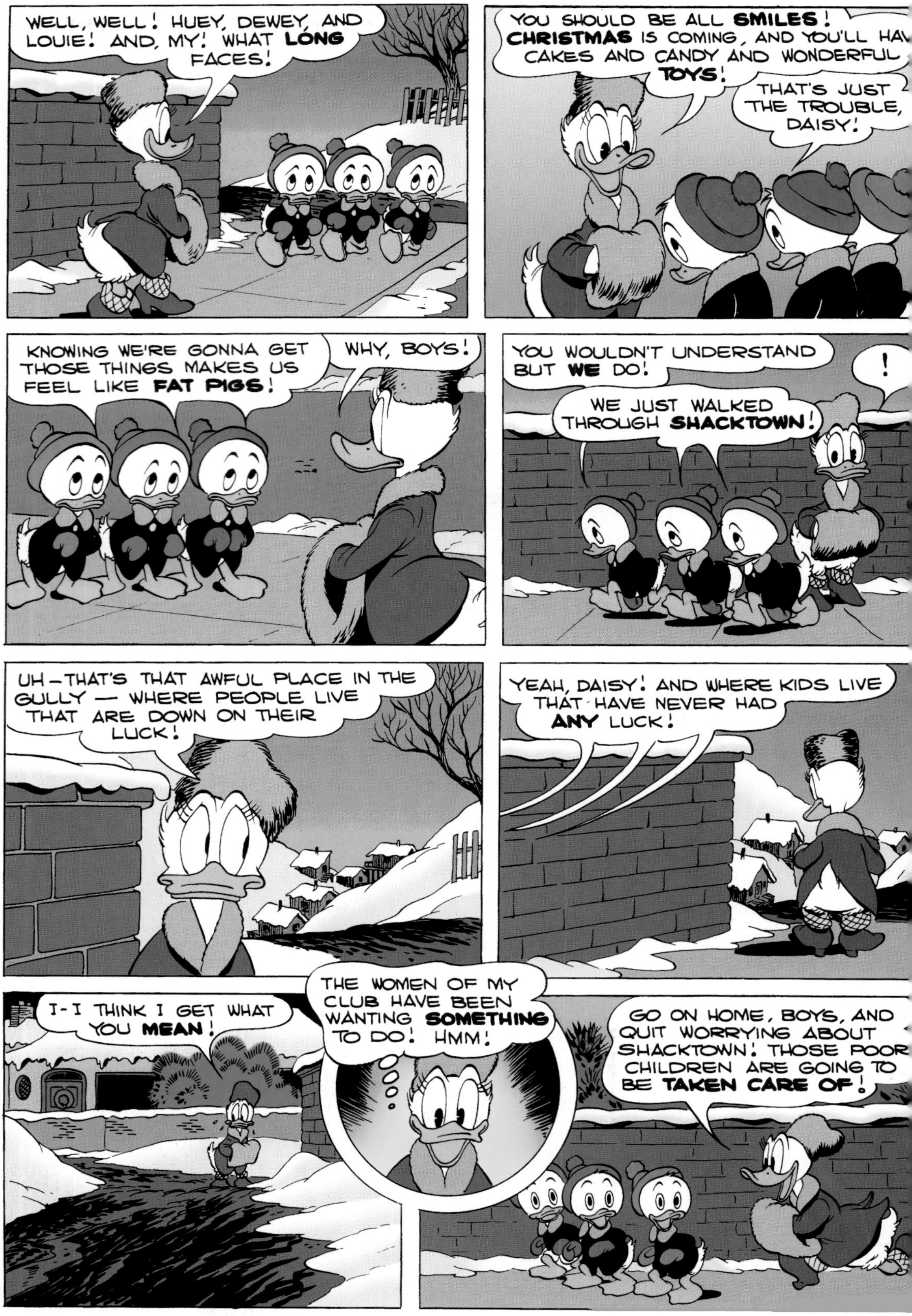

WELL, WELL! HUEY, DEWEY, AND LOUIE! AND, MY! WHAT **LONG** FACES!
YOU SHOULD BE ALL **SMILES**! **CHRISTMAS** IS COMING, AND YOU'LL HAV CAKES AND CANDY AND WONDERFUL **TOYS**!
THAT'S JUST THE TROUBLE, DAISY!
KNOWING WE'RE GONNA GET THOSE THINGS MAKES US FEEL LIKE **FAT PIGS**!
WHY, BOYS!
YOU WOULDN'T UNDERSTAND BUT **WE** DO!
!
WE JUST WALKED THROUGH **SHACKTOWN**!
UH—THAT'S THAT AWFUL PLACE IN THE GULLY — WHERE PEOPLE LIVE THAT ARE DOWN ON THEIR LUCK!
YEAH, DAISY! AND WHERE KIDS LIVE THAT HAVE NEVER HAD **ANY** LUCK!
I-I THINK I GET WHAT YOU **MEAN**!
THE WOMEN OF MY CLUB HAVE BEEN WANTING **SOMETHING** TO DO! HMM!
GO ON HOME, BOYS, AND QUIT WORRYING ABOUT SHACKTOWN! THOSE POOR CHILDREN ARE GOING TO BE **TAKEN CARE OF**!

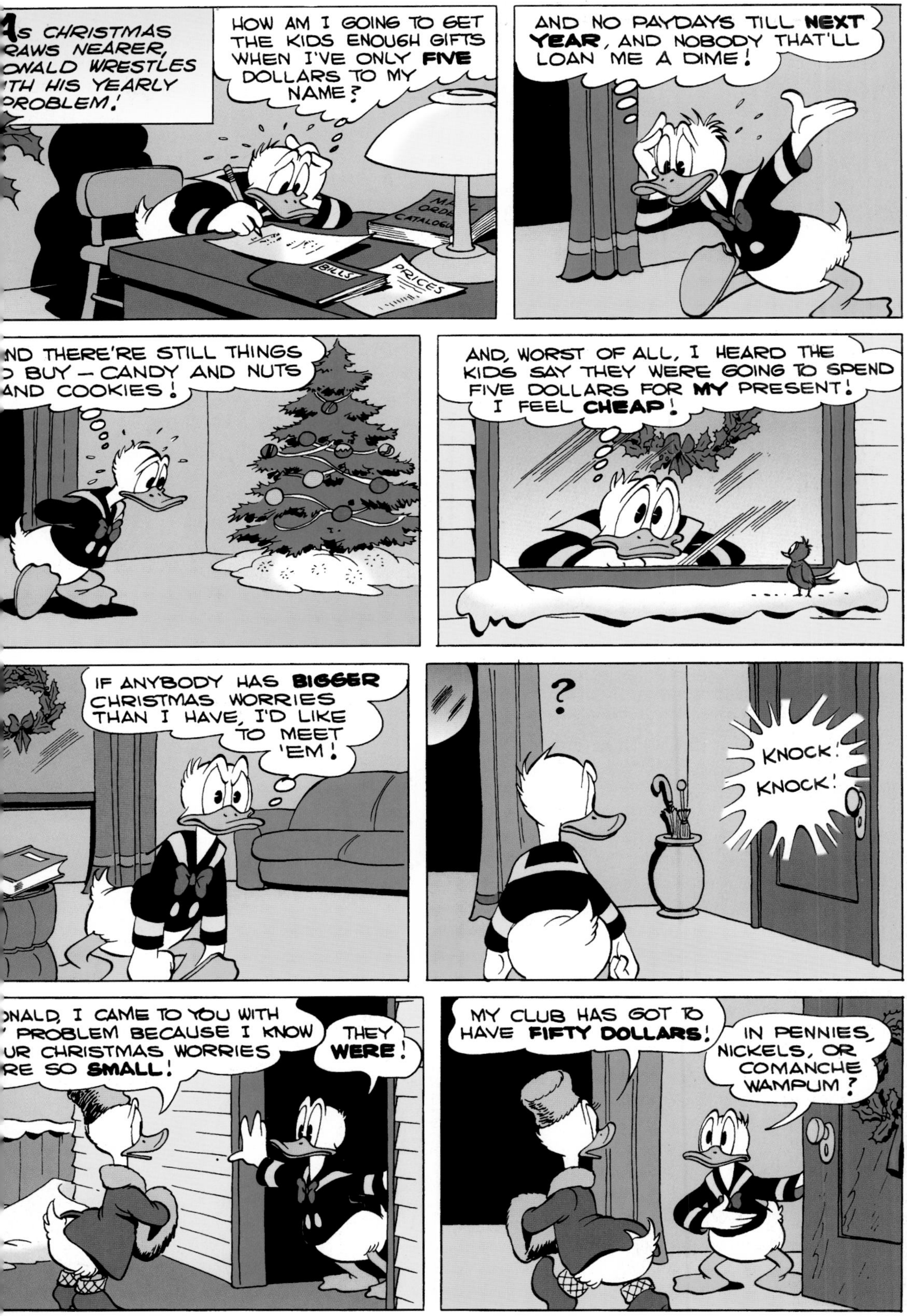
AS CHRISTMAS
RAWS NEARER,
ONALD WRESTLES
ITH HIS YEARLY
PROBLEM!
HOW AM I GOING TO GET THE KIDS ENOUGH GIFTS WHEN I'VE ONLY **FIVE** DOLLARS TO MY NAME?
BILLS
PRICES
AND NO PAYDAYS TILL **NEXT YEAR**, AND NOBODY THAT'LL LOAN ME A DIME!
ND THERE'RE STILL THINGS
BUY — CANDY AND NUTS
AND COOKIES!
AND, WORST OF ALL, I HEARD THE KIDS SAY THEY WERE GOING TO SPEND FIVE DOLLARS FOR **MY** PRESENT! I FEEL **CHEAP**!
IF ANYBODY HAS **BIGGER** CHRISTMAS WORRIES THAN I HAVE, I'D LIKE TO MEET 'EM!
?
KNOCK! KNOCK!
ONALD, I CAME TO YOU WITH
PROBLEM BECAUSE I KNOW
UR CHRISTMAS WORRIES
RE SO **SMALL**!
THEY **WERE**!
MY CLUB HAS GOT TO HAVE **FIFTY DOLLARS**!
IN PENNIES, NICKELS, OR COMANCHE WAMPUM?

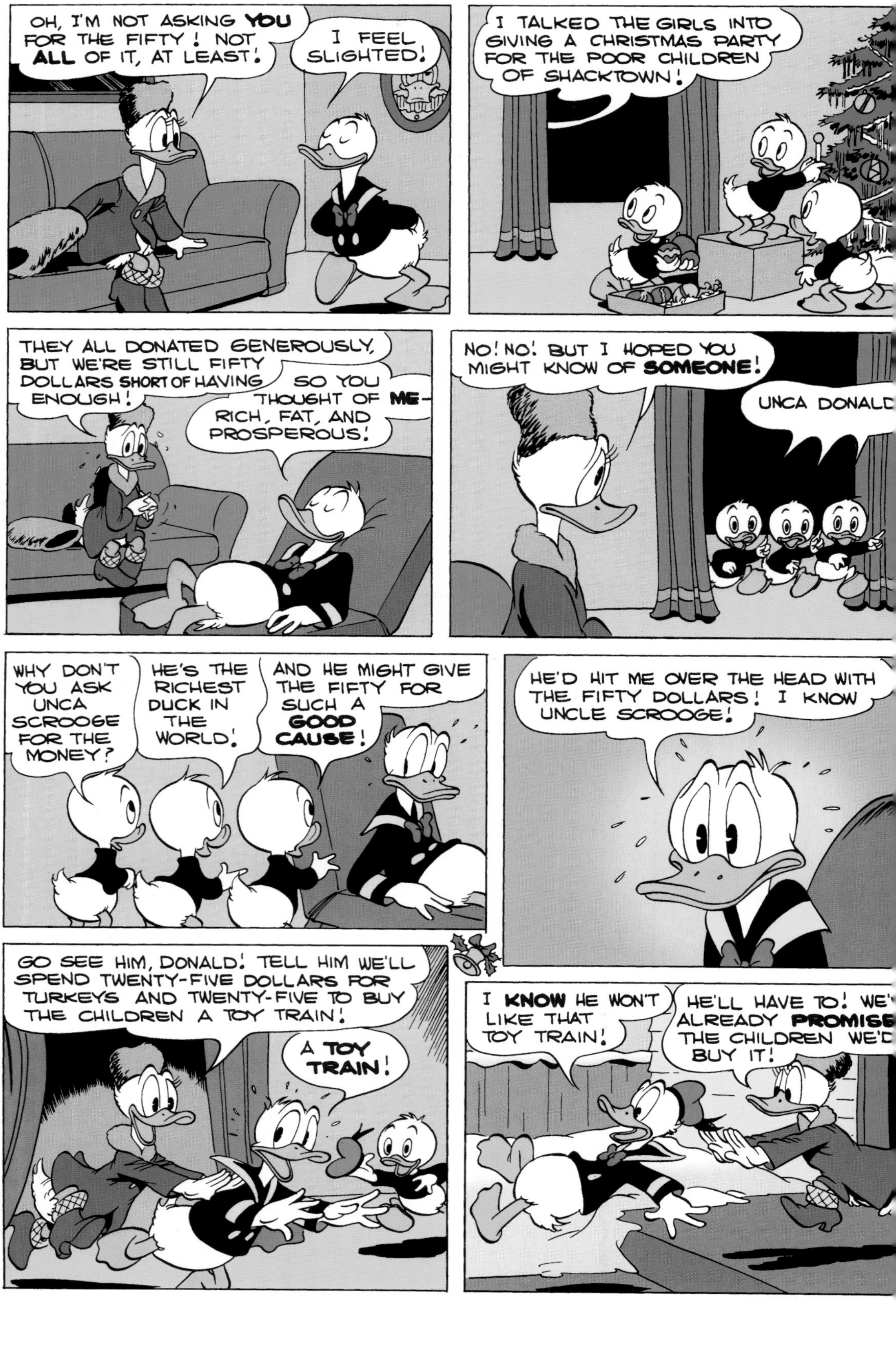
OH, I'M NOT ASKING **YOU** FOR THE FIFTY! NOT **ALL** OF IT, AT LEAST!
I FEEL SLIGHTED!
I TALKED THE GIRLS INTO GIVING A CHRISTMAS PARTY FOR THE POOR CHILDREN OF SHACKTOWN!
THEY ALL DONATED GENEROUSLY, BUT WE'RE STILL FIFTY DOLLARS **SHORT** OF HAVING ENOUGH!
SO YOU THOUGHT OF **ME**— RICH, FAT, AND PROSPEROUS!
NO! NO! BUT I HOPED YOU MIGHT KNOW OF **SOMEONE**!
UNCA DONALD
WHY DON'T YOU ASK UNCA SCROOGE FOR THE MONEY?
HE'S THE RICHEST DUCK IN THE WORLD!
AND HE MIGHT GIVE THE FIFTY FOR SUCH A **GOOD CAUSE**!
HE'D HIT ME OVER THE HEAD WITH THE FIFTY DOLLARS! I KNOW UNCLE SCROOGE!
GO SEE HIM, DONALD! TELL HIM WE'LL SPEND TWENTY-FIVE DOLLARS FOR TURKEYS AND TWENTY-FIVE TO BUY THE CHILDREN A TOY TRAIN!
A **TOY TRAIN**!
I **KNOW** HE WON'T LIKE THAT TOY TRAIN!
HE'LL HAVE TO! WE' ALREADY **PROMISE** THE CHILDREN WE'D BUY IT!

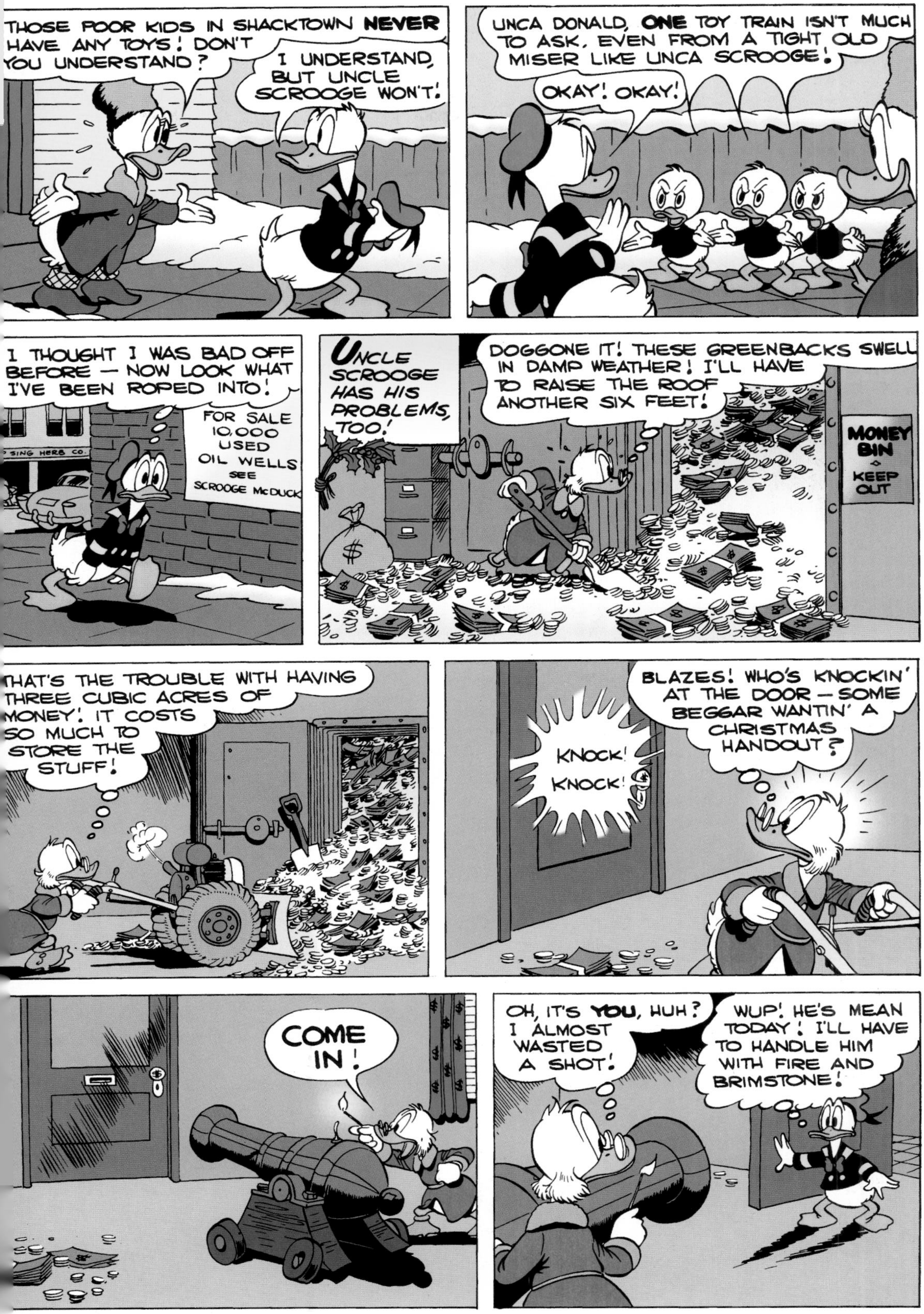
THOSE POOR KIDS IN SHACKTOWN NEVER HAVE ANY TOYS! DON'T YOU UNDERSTAND?
I UNDERSTAND, BUT UNCLE SCROOGE WON'T!
UNCA DONALD, ONE TOY TRAIN ISN'T MUCH TO ASK, EVEN FROM A TIGHT OLD MISER LIKE UNCA SCROOGE!
OKAY! OKAY!
I THOUGHT I WAS BAD OFF BEFORE — NOW LOOK WHAT I'VE BEEN ROPED INTO!
FOR SALE 10,000 USED OIL WELLS SEE SCROOGE McDUCK
SING HERB CO.
UNCLE SCROOGE HAS HIS PROBLEMS, TOO!
DOGGONE IT! THESE GREENBACKS SWELL IN DAMP WEATHER! I'LL HAVE TO RAISE THE ROOF ANOTHER SIX FEET!
MONEY BIN KEEP OUT
THAT'S THE TROUBLE WITH HAVING THREE CUBIC ACRES OF MONEY! IT COSTS SO MUCH TO STORE THE STUFF!
KNOCK! KNOCK!
BLAZES! WHO'S KNOCKIN' AT THE DOOR — SOME BEGGAR WANTIN' A CHRISTMAS HANDOUT?
COME IN!
OH, IT'S YOU, HUH? I ALMOST WASTED A SHOT!
WUP! HE'S MEAN TODAY! I'LL HAVE TO HANDLE HIM WITH FIRE AND BRIMSTONE!

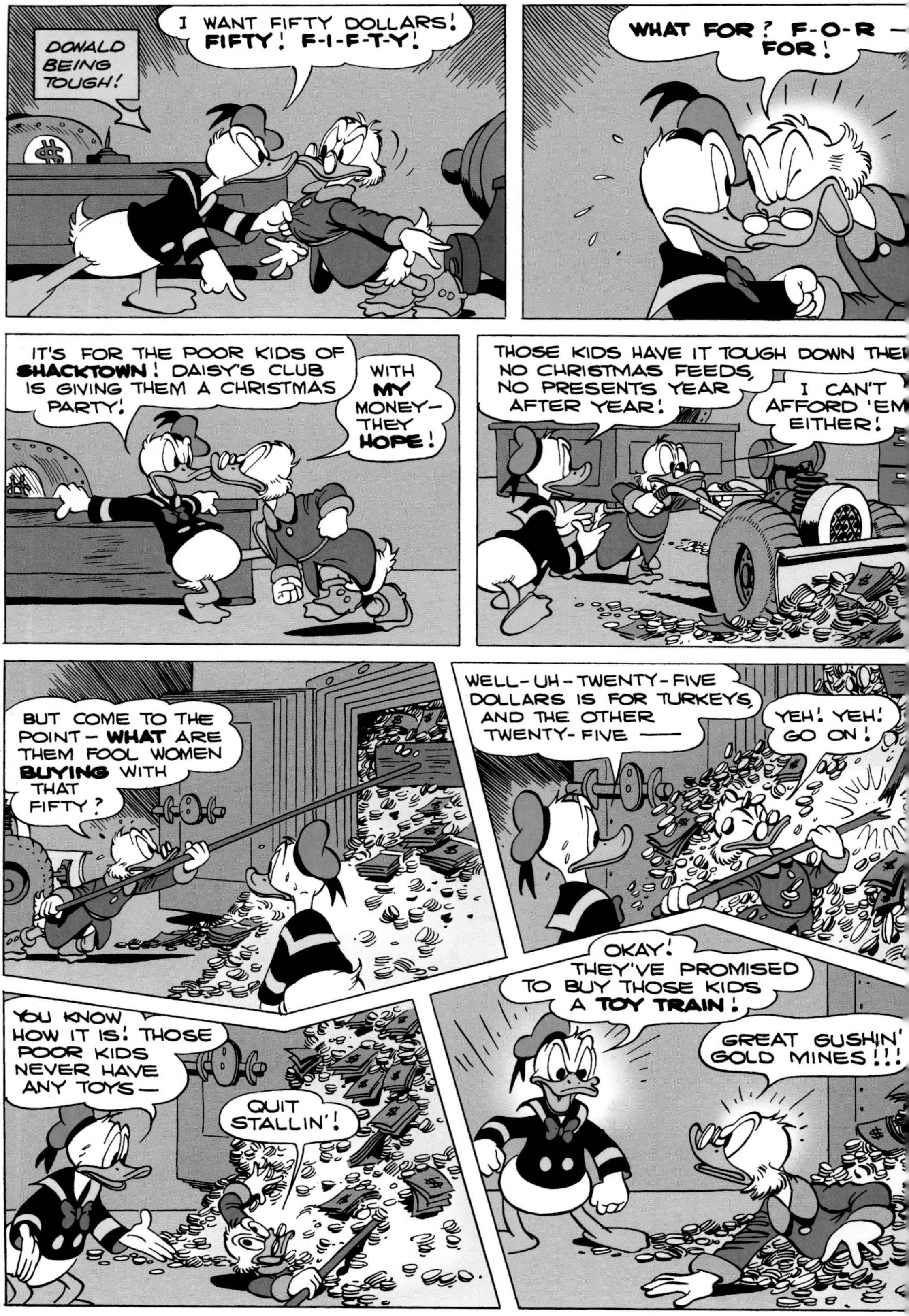
DONALD BEING TOUGH!
I WANT FIFTY DOLLARS! FIFTY! F-I-F-T-Y!
WHAT FOR? F-O-R — FOR!
IT'S FOR THE POOR KIDS OF SHACKTOWN! DAISY'S CLUB IS GIVING THEM A CHRISTMAS PARTY!
WITH MY MONEY— THEY HOPE!
THOSE KIDS HAVE IT TOUGH DOWN THE
NO CHRISTMAS FEEDS, NO PRESENTS YEAR AFTER YEAR!
I CAN'T AFFORD 'EM EITHER!
BUT COME TO THE POINT— WHAT ARE THEM FOOL WOMEN BUYING WITH THAT FIFTY?
WELL-UH-TWENTY-FIVE DOLLARS IS FOR TURKEYS, AND THE OTHER TWENTY-FIVE —
YEH! YEH! GO ON!
YOU KNOW HOW IT IS! THOSE POOR KIDS NEVER HAVE ANY TOYS—
QUIT STALLIN'!
OKAY! THEY'VE PROMISED TO BUY THOSE KIDS A TOY TRAIN!
GREAT GUSHIN' GOLD MINES!!!

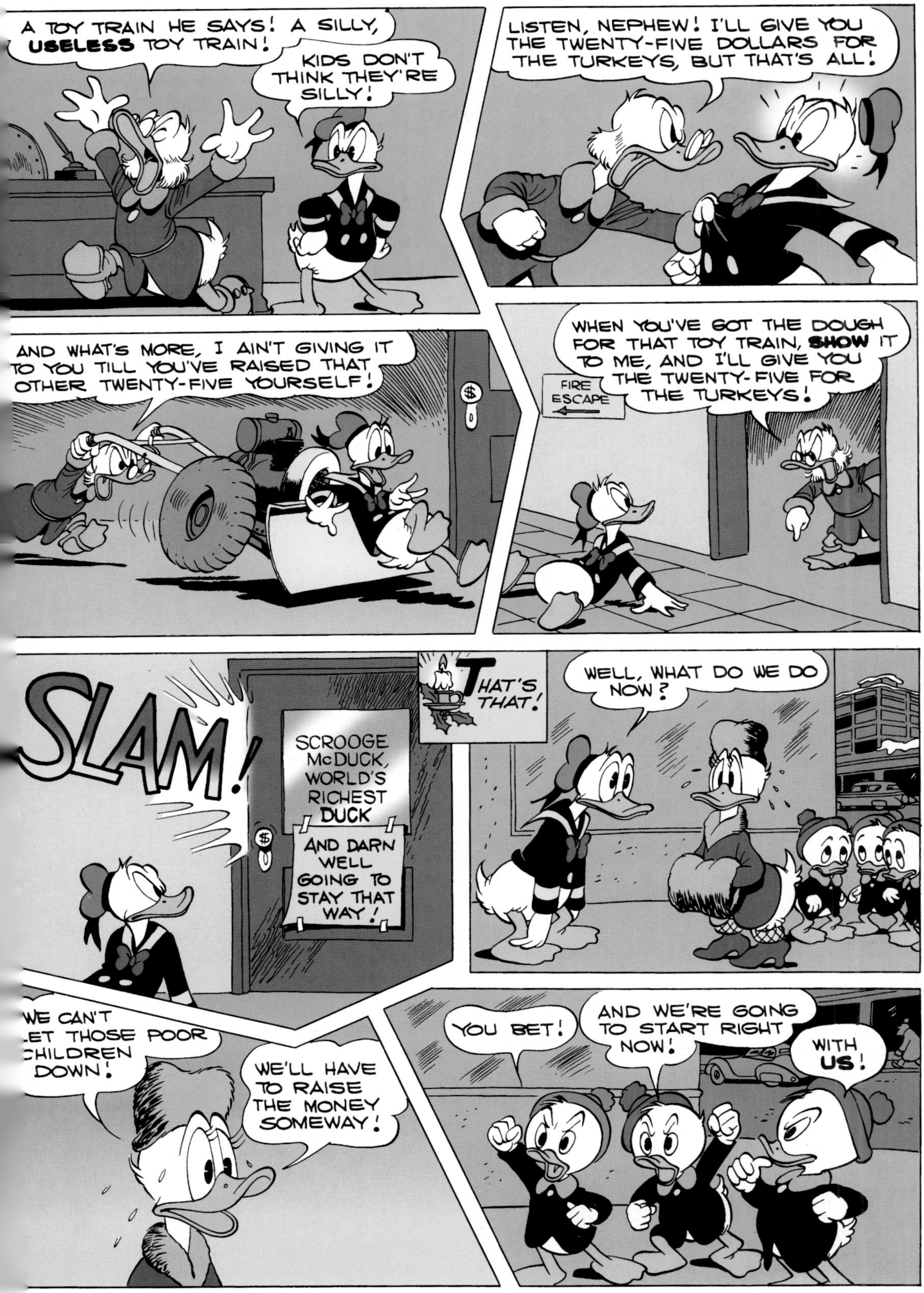
A TOY TRAIN HE SAYS! A SILLY, USELESS TOY TRAIN!
KIDS DON'T THINK THEY'RE SILLY!
LISTEN, NEPHEW! I'LL GIVE YOU THE TWENTY-FIVE DOLLARS FOR THE TURKEYS, BUT THAT'S ALL!
AND WHAT'S MORE, I AIN'T GIVING IT TO YOU TILL YOU'VE RAISED THAT OTHER TWENTY-FIVE YOURSELF!
WHEN YOU'VE GOT THE DOUGH FOR THAT TOY TRAIN, SHOW IT TO ME, AND I'LL GIVE YOU THE TWENTY-FIVE FOR THE TURKEYS!
FIRE ESCAPE
SLAM!
SCROOGE McDUCK, WORLD'S RICHEST DUCK
AND DARN WELL GOING TO STAY THAT WAY!
THAT'S THAT!
WELL, WHAT DO WE DO NOW?
WE CAN'T LET THOSE POOR CHILDREN DOWN!
WE'LL HAVE TO RAISE THE MONEY SOMEWAY!
YOU BET!
AND WE'RE GOING TO START RIGHT NOW!
WITH US!

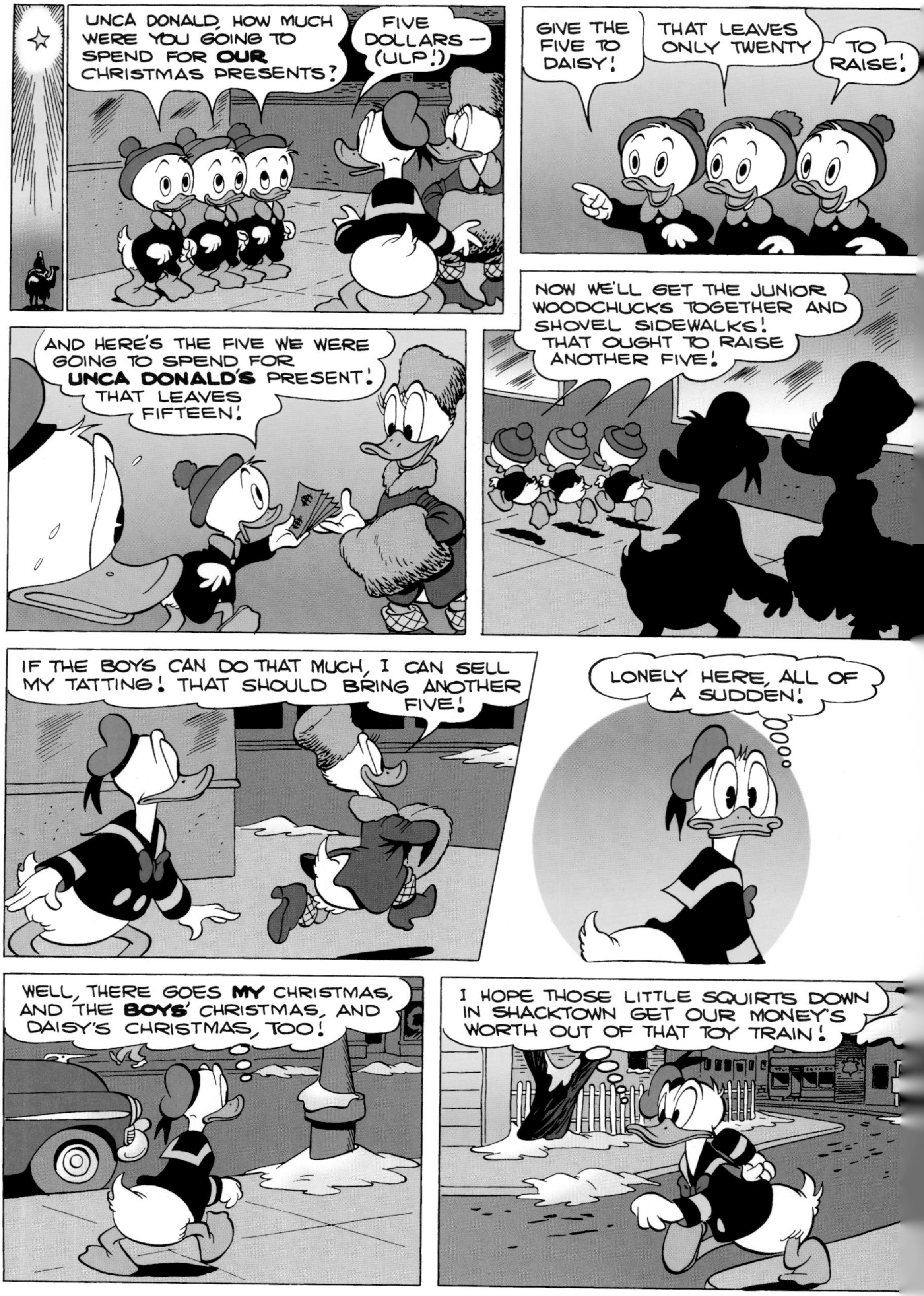
UNCA DONALD, HOW MUCH WERE YOU GOING TO SPEND FOR OUR CHRISTMAS PRESENTS?
FIVE DOLLARS— (ULP!)
GIVE THE FIVE TO DAISY!
THAT LEAVES ONLY TWENTY
TO RAISE!
AND HERE'S THE FIVE WE WERE GOING TO SPEND FOR UNCA DONALD'S PRESENT! THAT LEAVES FIFTEEN!
NOW WE'LL GET THE JUNIOR WOODCHUCKS TOGETHER AND SHOVEL SIDEWALKS! THAT OUGHT TO RAISE ANOTHER FIVE!
IF THE BOYS CAN DO THAT MUCH, I CAN SELL MY TATTING! THAT SHOULD BRING ANOTHER FIVE!
LONELY HERE, ALL OF A SUDDEN!
WELL, THERE GOES MY CHRISTMAS, AND THE BOYS' CHRISTMAS, AND DAISY'S CHRISTMAS, TOO!
I HOPE THOSE LITTLE SQUIRTS DOWN IN SHACKTOWN GET OUR MONEY'S WORTH OUT OF THAT TOY TRAIN!

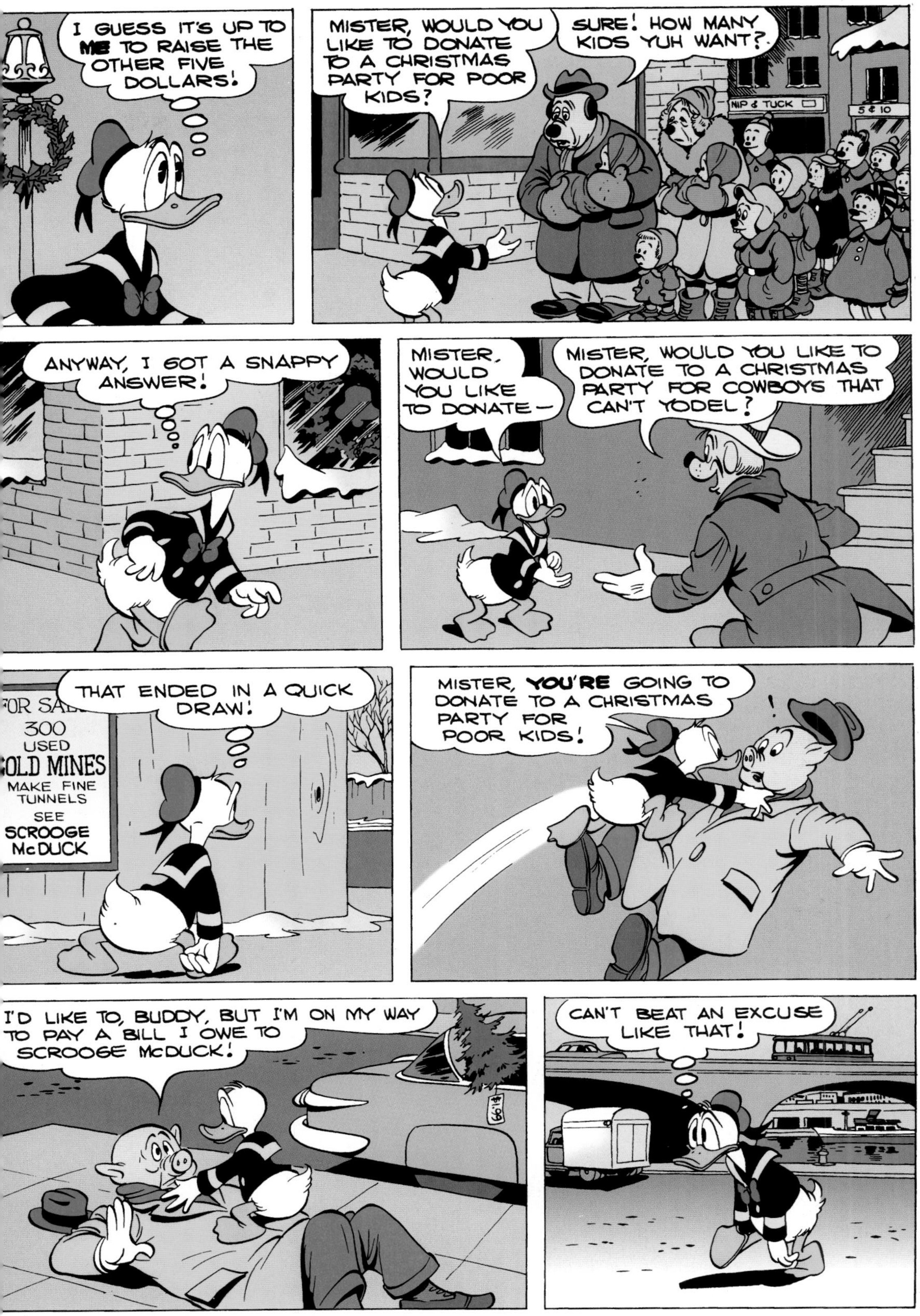
I GUESS IT'S UP TO ME TO RAISE THE OTHER FIVE DOLLARS!
MISTER, WOULD YOU LIKE TO DONATE TO A CHRISTMAS PARTY FOR POOR KIDS?
SURE! HOW MANY KIDS YUH WANT?
NIP & TUCK
5 ¢ 10
ANYWAY, I GOT A SNAPPY ANSWER!
MISTER, WOULD YOU LIKE TO DONATE—
MISTER, WOULD YOU LIKE TO DONATE TO A CHRISTMAS PARTY FOR COWBOYS THAT CAN'T YODEL?
THAT ENDED IN A QUICK DRAW!
300 USED
MAKE FINE TUNNELS
SEE SCROOGE McDUCK
MISTER, YOU'RE GOING TO DONATE TO A CHRISTMAS PARTY FOR POOR KIDS!
I'D LIKE TO, BUDDY, BUT I'M ON MY WAY TO PAY A BILL I OWE TO SCROOGE McDUCK!
CAN'T BEAT AN EXCUSE LIKE THAT!

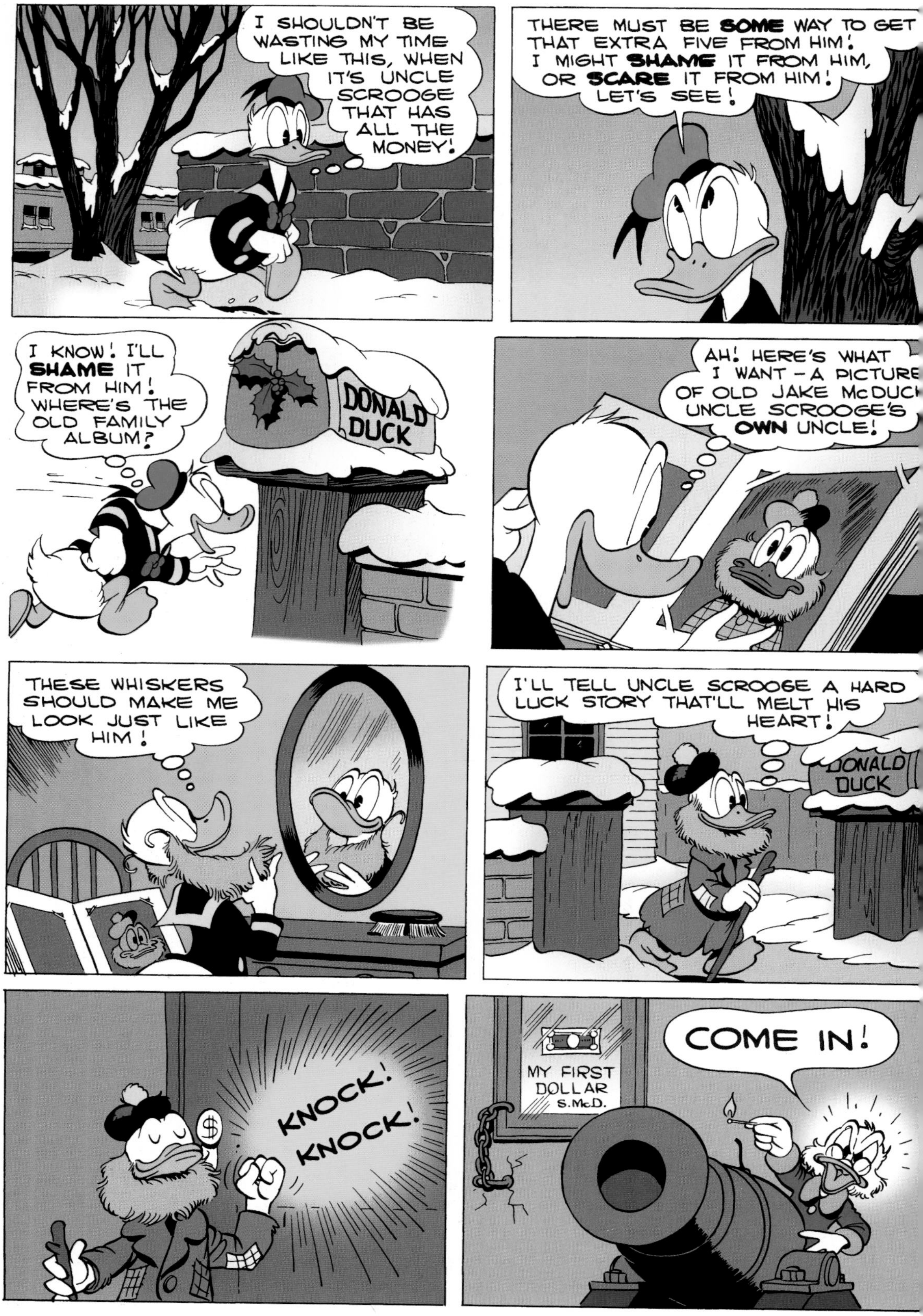
I SHOULDN'T BE WASTING MY TIME LIKE THIS, WHEN IT'S UNCLE SCROOGE THAT HAS ALL THE MONEY!
THERE MUST BE SOME WAY TO GET THAT EXTRA FIVE FROM HIM! I MIGHT SHAME IT FROM HIM, OR SCARE IT FROM HIM! LET'S SEE!
I KNOW! I'LL SHAME IT FROM HIM! WHERE'S THE OLD FAMILY ALBUM?
DONALD DUCK
AH! HERE'S WHAT I WANT — A PICTURE OF OLD JAKE McDUCK UNCLE SCROOGE'S OWN UNCLE!
THESE WHISKERS SHOULD MAKE ME LOOK JUST LIKE HIM!
I'LL TELL UNCLE SCROOGE A HARD LUCK STORY THAT'LL MELT HIS HEART!
DONALD DUCK
KNOCK! KNOCK!
MY FIRST DOLLAR S.McD.
COME IN!

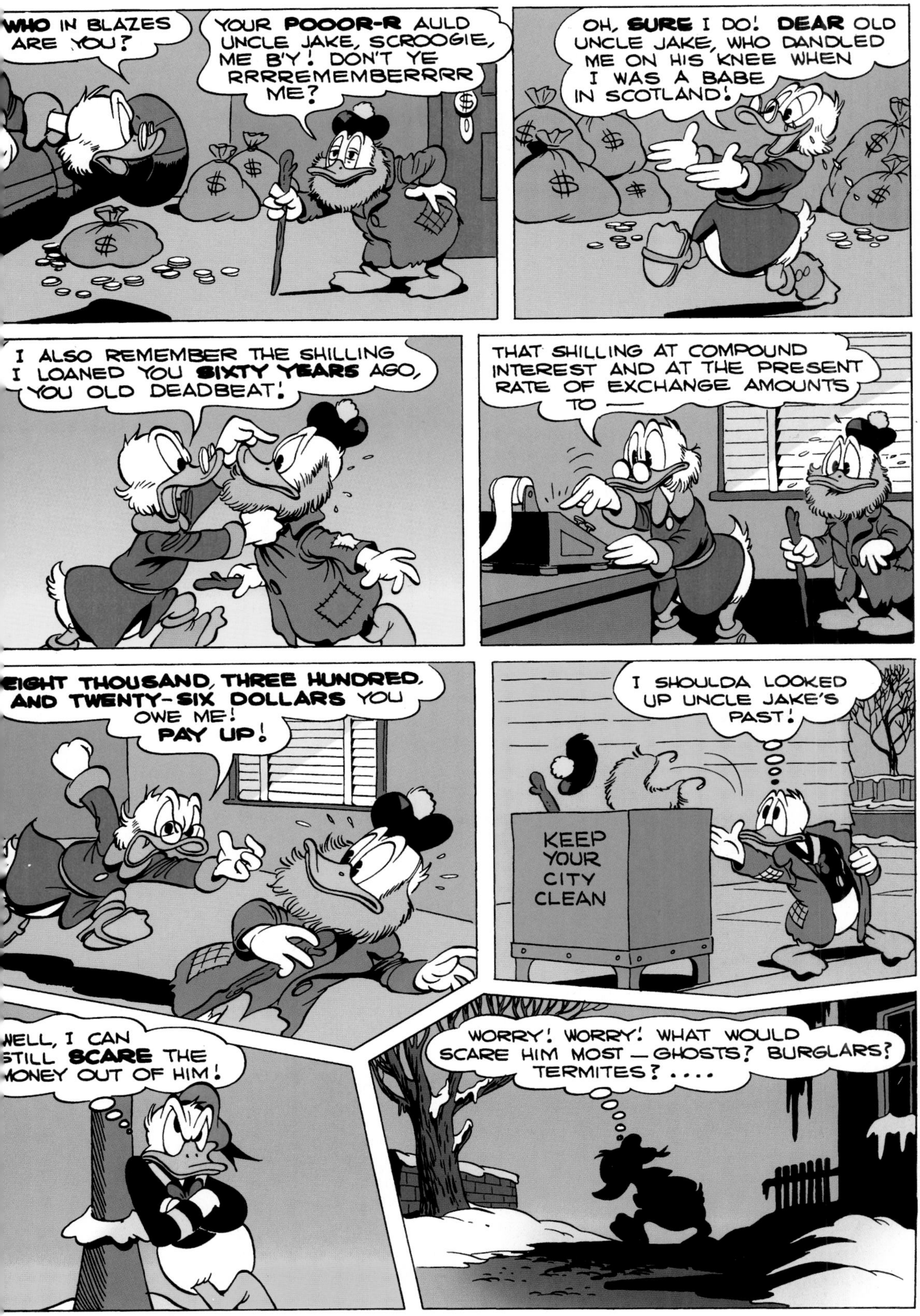
WHO IN BLAZES ARE YOU?
YOUR POOOR-R AULD UNCLE JAKE, SCROOGIE, ME B'Y! DON'T YE RRRREMEMBERRRR ME?
OH, SURE I DO! DEAR OLD UNCLE JAKE, WHO DANDLED ME ON HIS KNEE WHEN I WAS A BABE IN SCOTLAND!
I ALSO REMEMBER THE SHILLING I LOANED YOU SIXTY YEARS AGO, YOU OLD DEADBEAT!
THAT SHILLING AT COMPOUND INTEREST AND AT THE PRESENT RATE OF EXCHANGE AMOUNTS TO —
EIGHT THOUSAND, THREE HUNDRED, AND TWENTY-SIX DOLLARS YOU OWE ME! PAY UP!
I SHOULDA LOOKED UP UNCLE JAKE'S PAST!
KEEP YOUR CITY CLEAN
WELL, I CAN STILL SCARE THE MONEY OUT OF HIM!
WORRY! WORRY! WHAT WOULD SCARE HIM MOST — GHOSTS? BURGLARS? TERMITES? . . . .

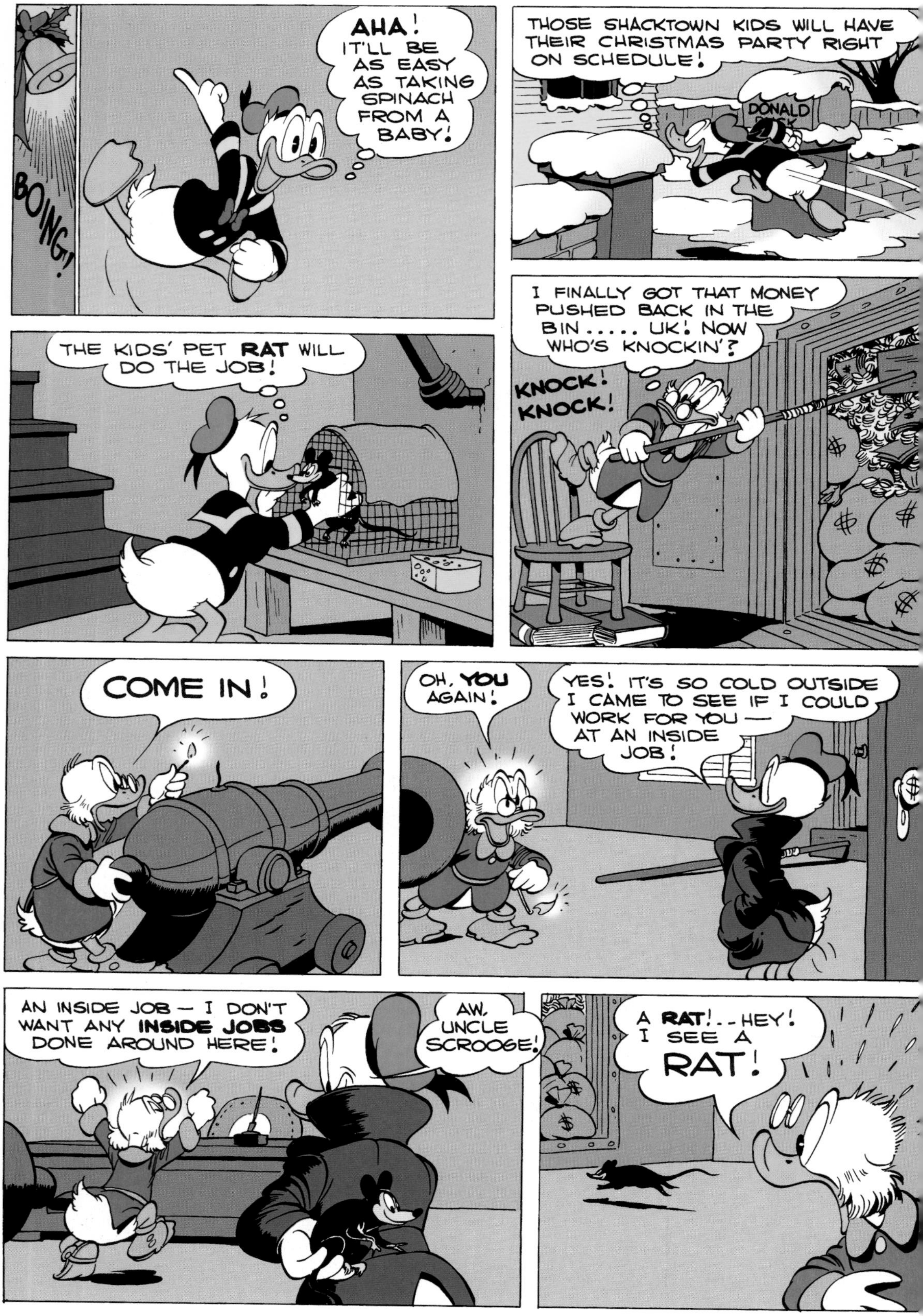
BOING!!
AHA! IT'LL BE AS EASY AS TAKING SPINACH FROM A BABY!
THOSE SHACKTOWN KIDS WILL HAVE THEIR CHRISTMAS PARTY RIGHT ON SCHEDULE!
THE KIDS' PET RAT WILL DO THE JOB!
I FINALLY GOT THAT MONEY PUSHED BACK IN THE BIN ..... UK! NOW WHO'S KNOCKIN'?
KNOCK! KNOCK!
COME IN!
OH, YOU AGAIN!
YES! IT'S SO COLD OUTSIDE I CAME TO SEE IF I COULD WORK FOR YOU — AT AN INSIDE JOB!
AN INSIDE JOB — I DON'T WANT ANY INSIDE JOBS DONE AROUND HERE!
AW, UNCLE SCROOGE!
A RAT!--HEY! I SEE A RAT!

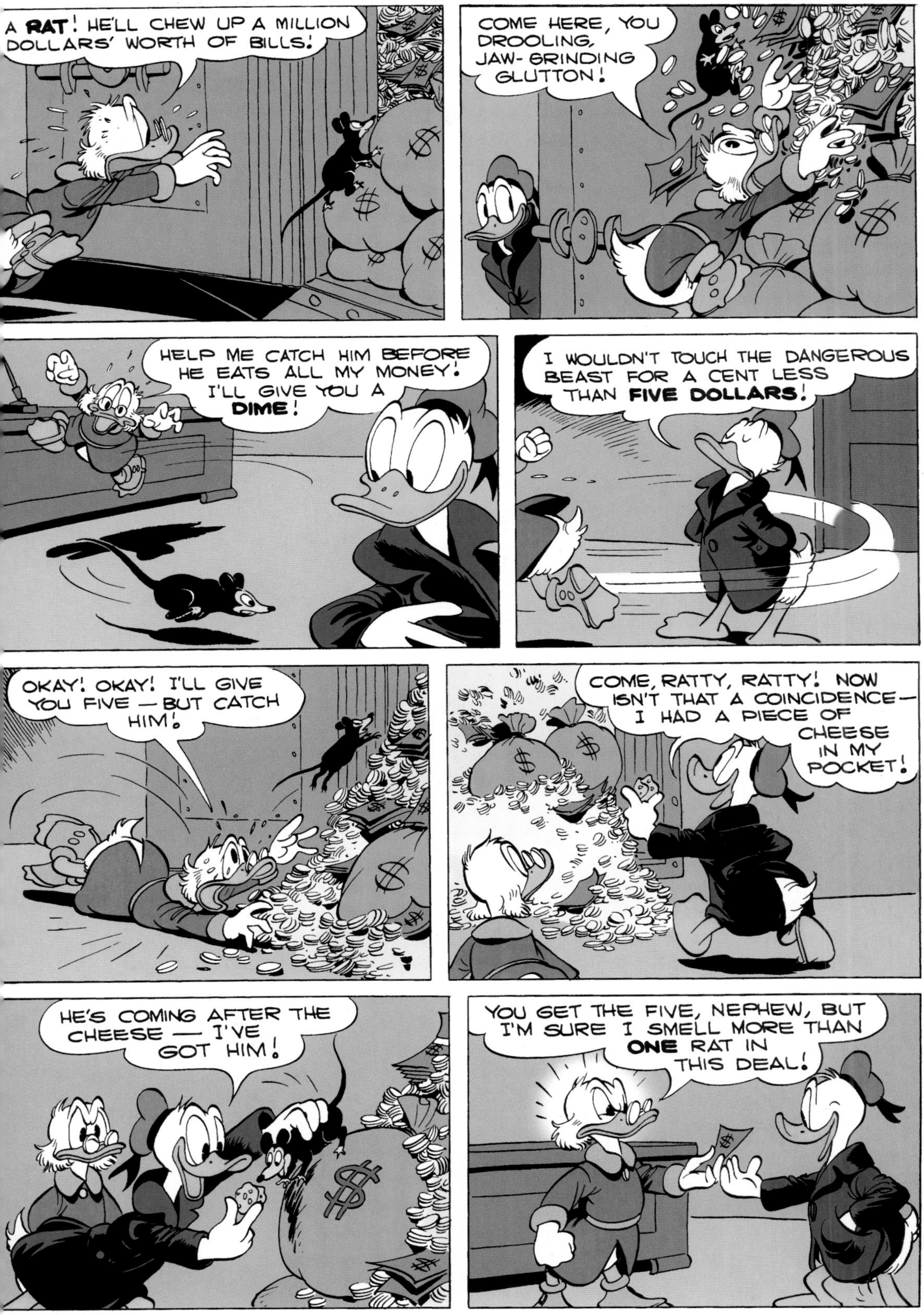
A RAT! HE'LL CHEW UP A MILLION DOLLARS' WORTH OF BILLS!
COME HERE, YOU DROOLING, JAW-GRINDING GLUTTON!
HELP ME CATCH HIM BEFORE HE EATS ALL MY MONEY! I'LL GIVE YOU A DIME!
I WOULDN'T TOUCH THE DANGEROUS BEAST FOR A CENT LESS THAN FIVE DOLLARS!
OKAY! OKAY! I'LL GIVE YOU FIVE — BUT CATCH HIM!
COME, RATTY, RATTY! NOW ISN'T THAT A COINCIDENCE— I HAD A PIECE OF CHEESE IN MY POCKET!
HE'S COMING AFTER THE CHEESE — I'VE GOT HIM!
YOU GET THE FIVE, NEPHEW, BUT I'M SURE I SMELL MORE THAN ONE RAT IN THIS DEAL!

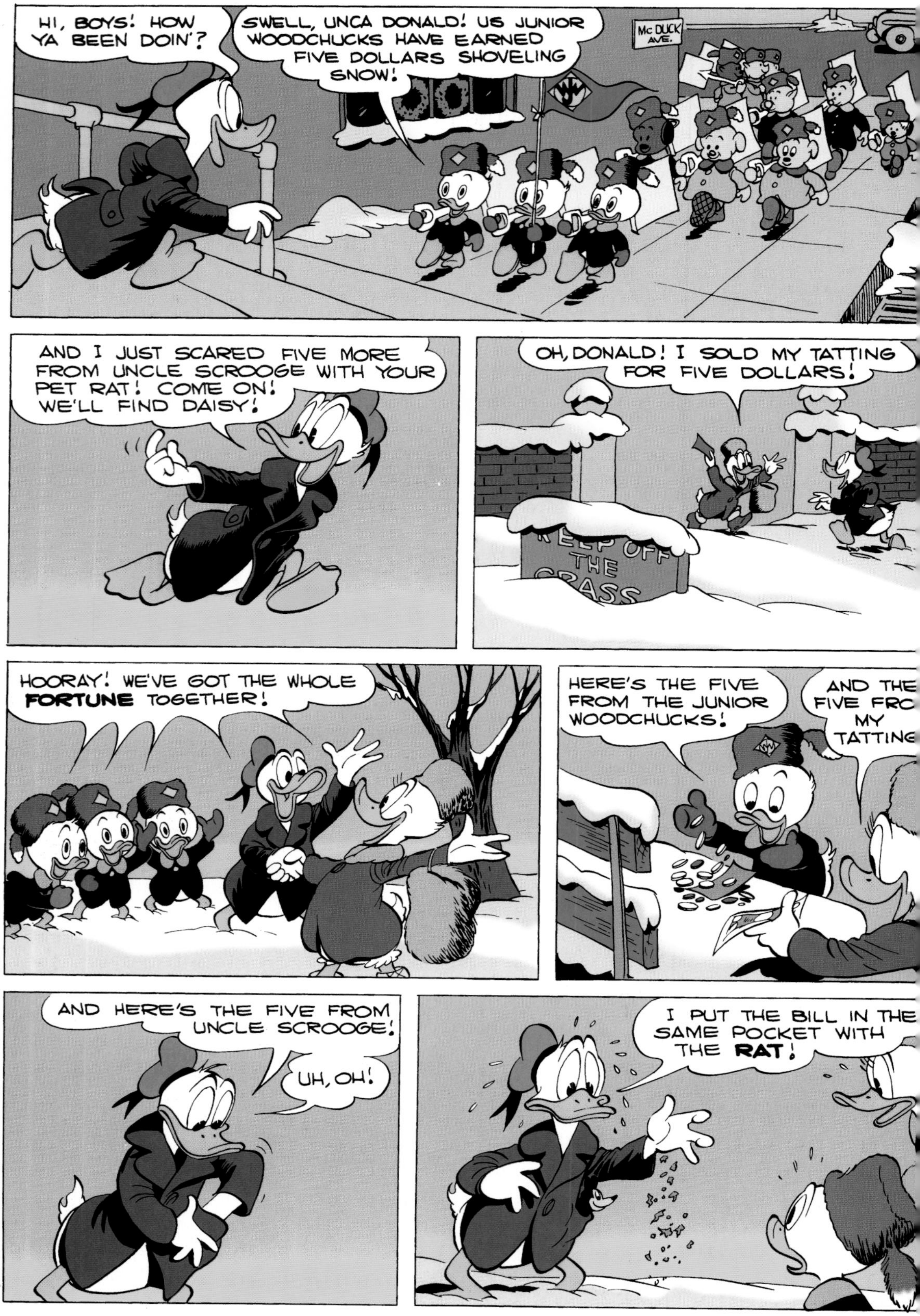

HI, BOYS! HOW YA BEEN DOIN'?
SWELL, UNCA DONALD! US JUNIOR WOODCHUCKS HAVE EARNED FIVE DOLLARS SHOVELING SNOW!
Mc DUCK AVE.
AND I JUST SCARED FIVE MORE FROM UNCLE SCROOGE WITH YOUR PET RAT! COME ON! WE'LL FIND DAISY!
OH, DONALD! I SOLD MY TATTING FOR FIVE DOLLARS!
THE
HOORAY! WE'VE GOT THE WHOLE **FORTUNE** TOGETHER!
HERE'S THE FIVE FROM THE JUNIOR WOODCHUCKS!
AND THE FIVE FRO MY TATTING
AND HERE'S THE FIVE FROM UNCLE SCROOGE!
UH, OH!
I PUT THE BILL IN THE SAME POCKET WITH THE **RAT**!

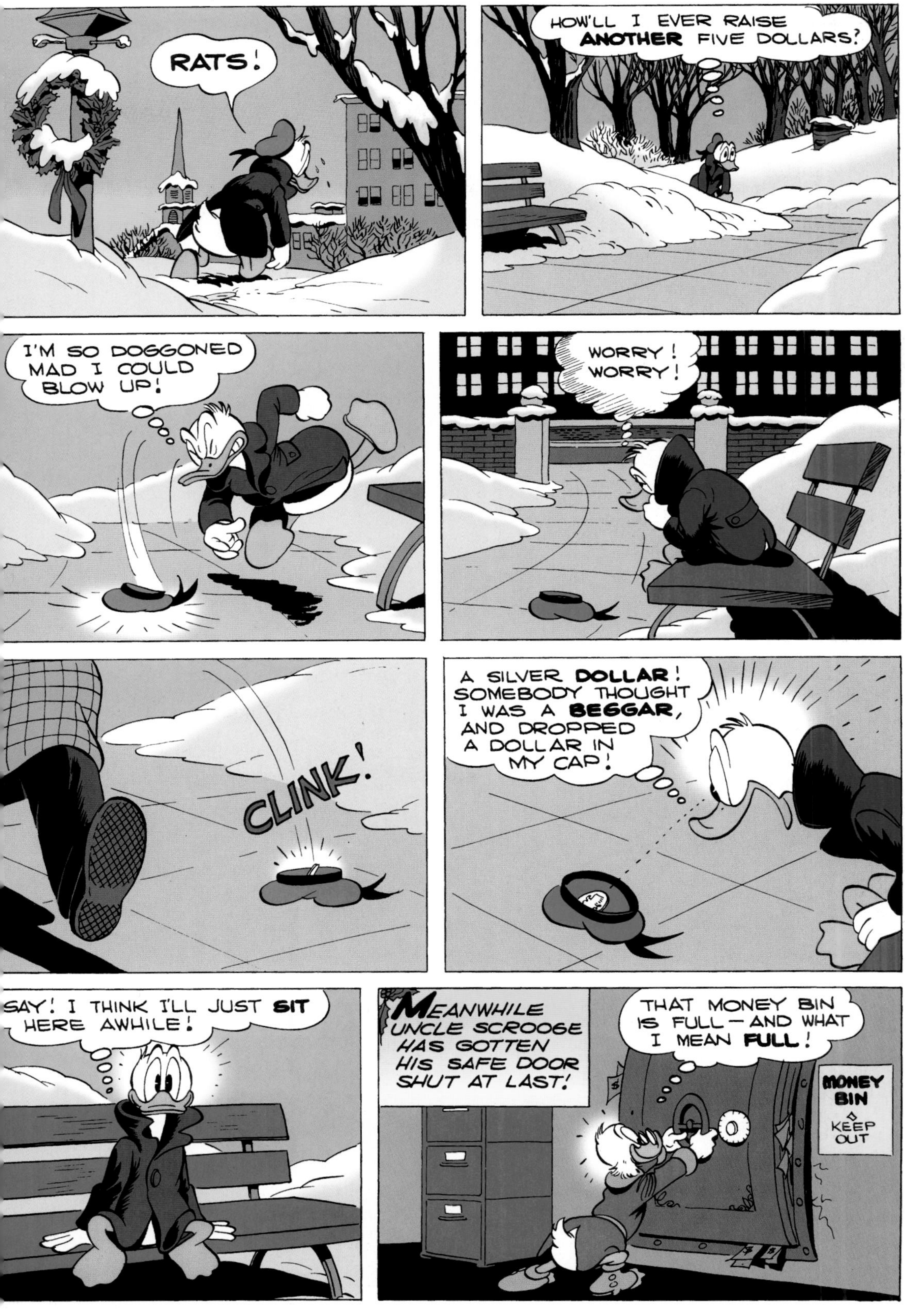
RATS!
HOW'LL I EVER RAISE ANOTHER FIVE DOLLARS?
I'M SO DOGGONED MAD I COULD BLOW UP!
WORRY! WORRY!
CLINK!
A SILVER DOLLAR! SOMEBODY THOUGHT I WAS A BEGGAR, AND DROPPED A DOLLAR IN MY CAP!
SAY! I THINK I'LL JUST SIT HERE AWHILE!
MEANWHILE UNCLE SCROOGE HAS GOTTEN HIS SAFE DOOR SHUT AT LAST!
THAT MONEY BIN IS FULL—AND WHAT I MEAN FULL!
MONEY BIN KEEP OUT

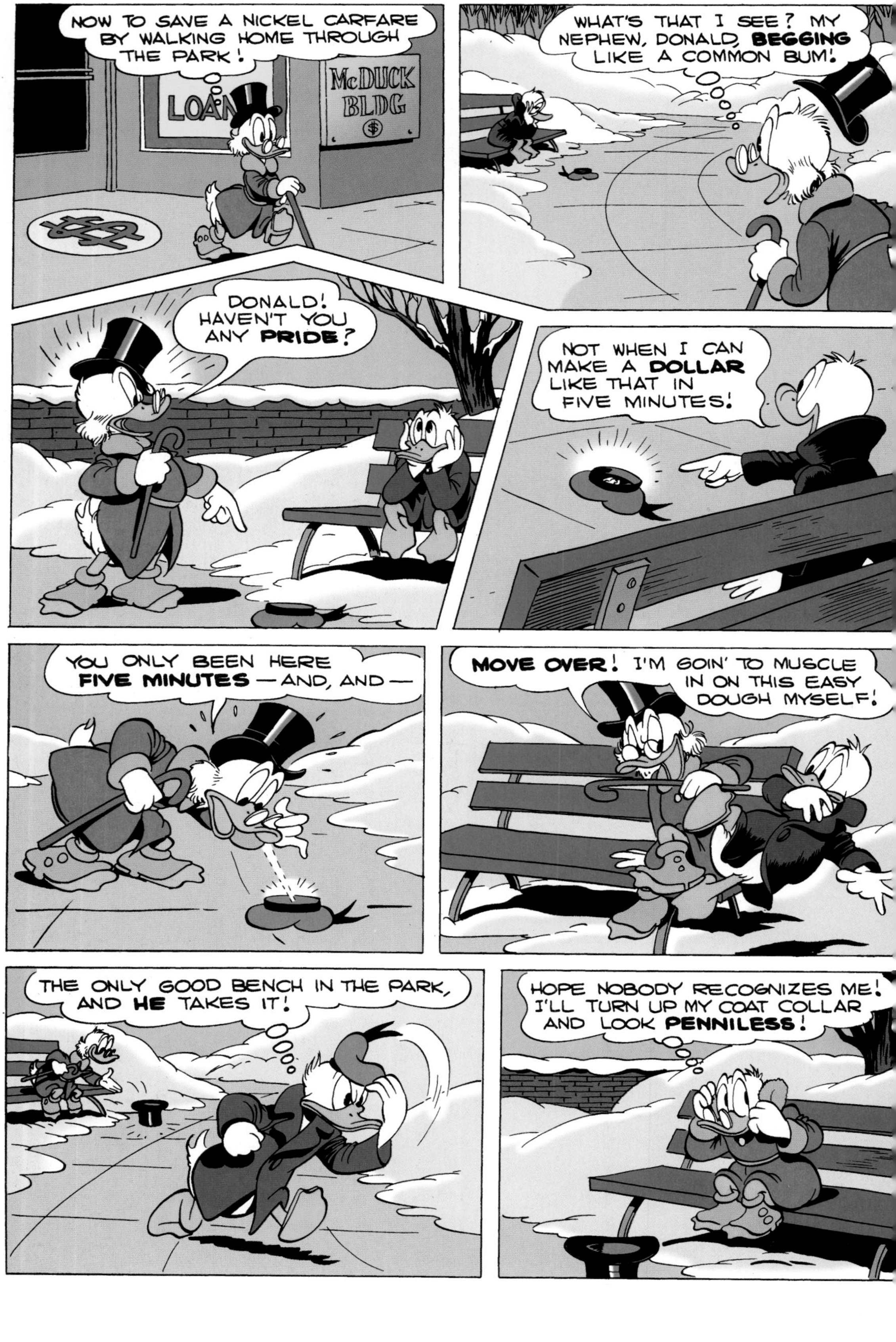
NOW TO SAVE A NICKEL CARFARE BY WALKING HOME THROUGH THE PARK!
LOAN
McDUCK BLDG
WHAT'S THAT I SEE? MY NEPHEW, DONALD, BEGGING LIKE A COMMON BUM!
DONALD! HAVEN'T YOU ANY PRIDE?
NOT WHEN I CAN MAKE A DOLLAR LIKE THAT IN FIVE MINUTES!
YOU ONLY BEEN HERE FIVE MINUTES — AND, AND —
MOVE OVER! I'M GOIN' TO MUSCLE IN ON THIS EASY DOUGH MYSELF!
THE ONLY GOOD BENCH IN THE PARK, AND HE TAKES IT!
HOPE NOBODY RECOGNIZES ME! I'LL TURN UP MY COAT COLLAR AND LOOK PENNILESS!

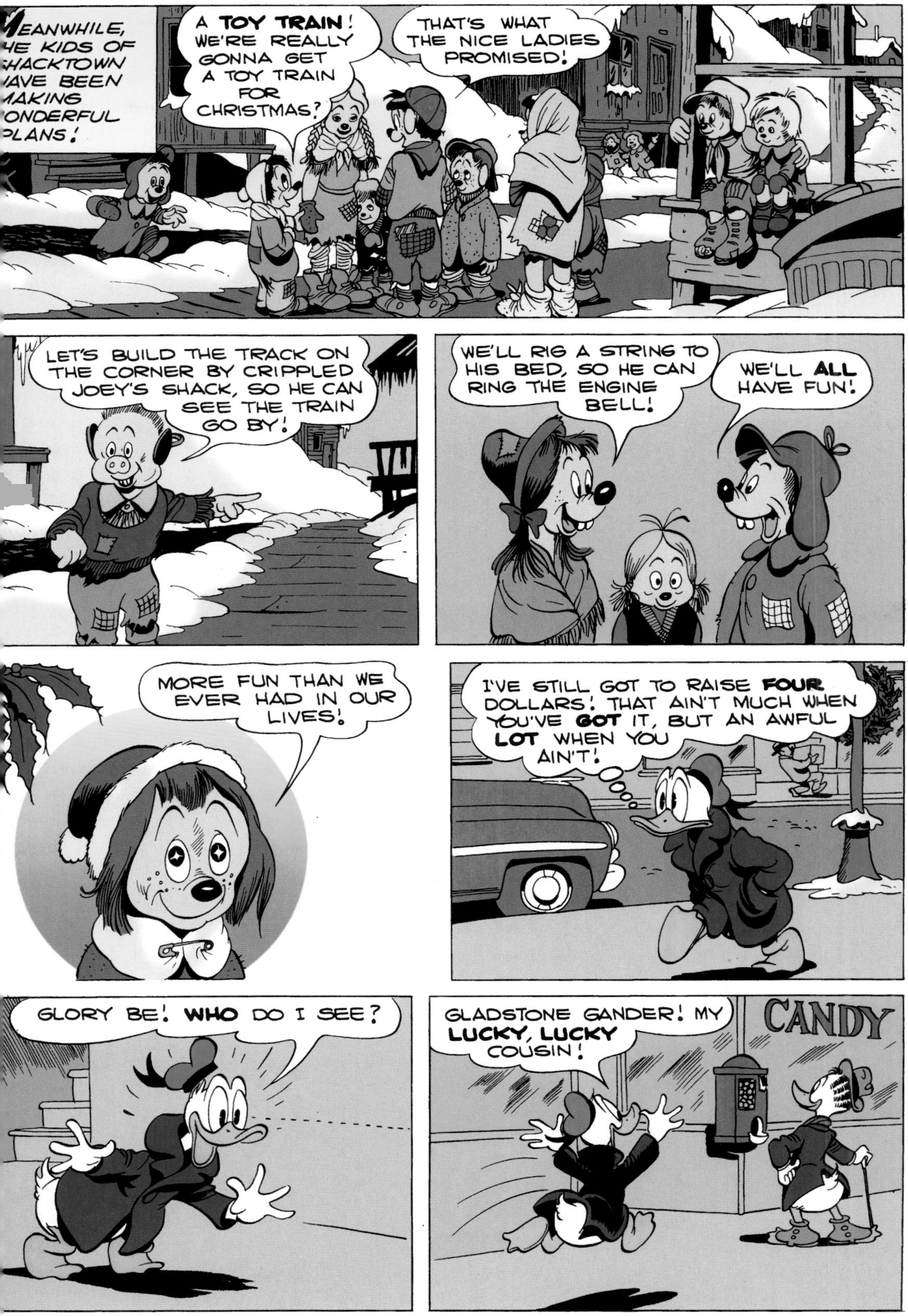
MEANWHILE, THE KIDS OF SHACKTOWN HAVE BEEN MAKING WONDERFUL PLANS!
A TOY TRAIN! WE'RE REALLY GONNA GET A TOY TRAIN FOR CHRISTMAS?
THAT'S WHAT THE NICE LADIES PROMISED!
LET'S BUILD THE TRACK ON THE CORNER BY CRIPPLED JOEY'S SHACK, SO HE CAN SEE THE TRAIN GO BY!
WE'LL RIG A STRING TO HIS BED, SO HE CAN RING THE ENGINE BELL!
WE'LL ALL HAVE FUN!
MORE FUN THAN WE EVER HAD IN OUR LIVES!
I'VE STILL GOT TO RAISE FOUR DOLLARS! THAT AIN'T MUCH WHEN YOU'VE GOT IT, BUT AN AWFUL LOT WHEN YOU AIN'T!
GLORY BE! WHO DO I SEE?
GLADSTONE GANDER! MY LUCKY, LUCKY COUSIN!
CANDY

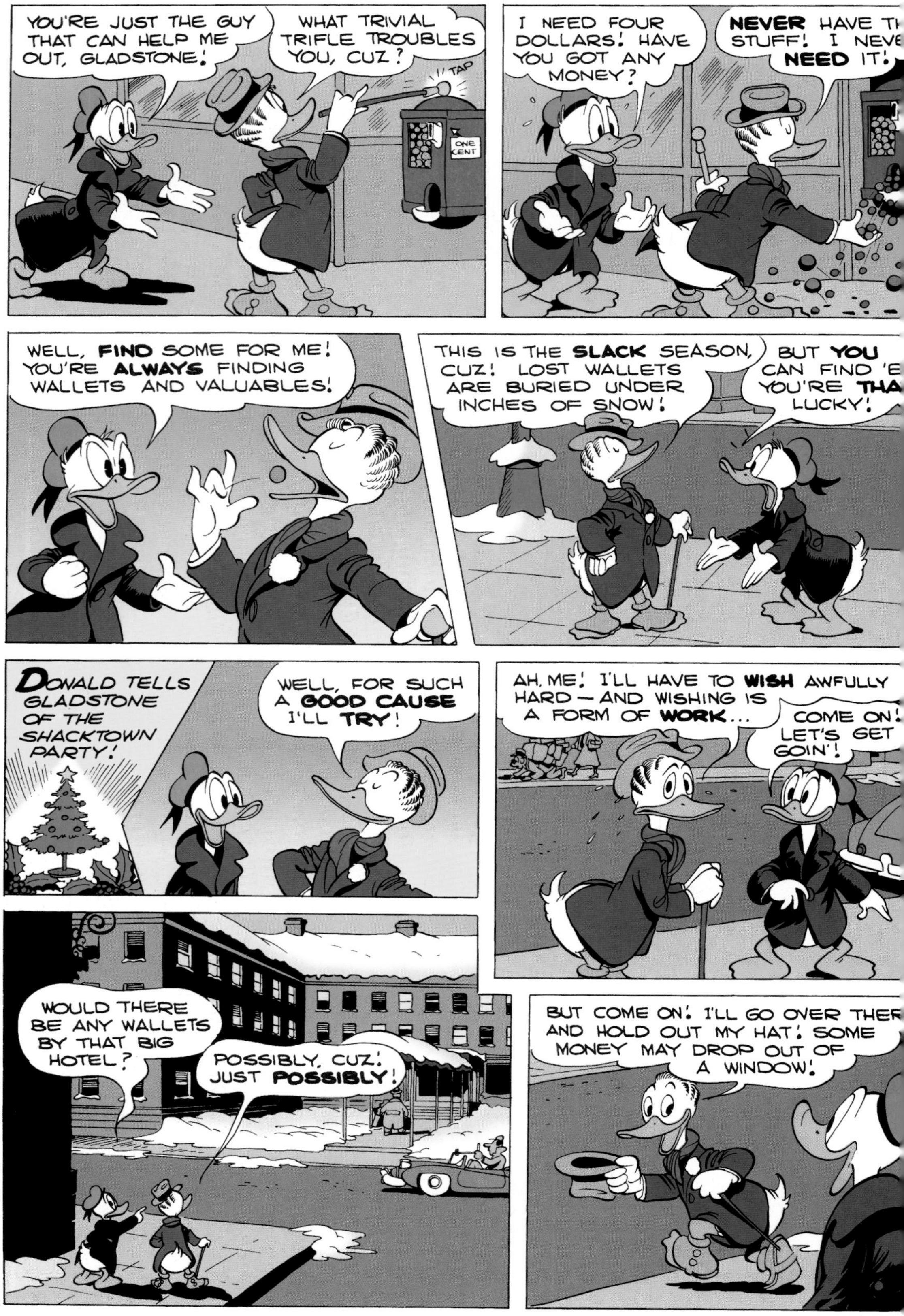

YOU'RE JUST THE GUY THAT CAN HELP ME OUT, GLADSTONE!
WHAT TRIVIAL TRIFLE TROUBLES YOU, CUZ?
TAP
ONE CENT
I NEED FOUR DOLLARS! HAVE YOU GOT ANY MONEY?
NEVER HAVE TH STUFF! I NEVE NEED IT!
WELL, FIND SOME FOR ME! YOU'RE ALWAYS FINDING WALLETS AND VALUABLES!
THIS IS THE SLACK SEASON, CUZ! LOST WALLETS ARE BURIED UNDER INCHES OF SNOW!
BUT YOU CAN FIND 'E YOU'RE THA LUCKY!
DONALD TELLS GLADSTONE OF THE SHACKTOWN PARTY!
WELL, FOR SUCH A GOOD CAUSE I'LL TRY!
AH, ME! I'LL HAVE TO WISH AWFULLY HARD — AND WISHING IS A FORM OF WORK...
COME ON! LET'S GET GOIN'!
WOULD THERE BE ANY WALLETS BY THAT BIG HOTEL?
POSSIBLY, CUZ! JUST POSSIBLY!
BUT COME ON! I'LL GO OVER THER AND HOLD OUT MY HAT! SOME MONEY MAY DROP OUT OF A WINDOW!

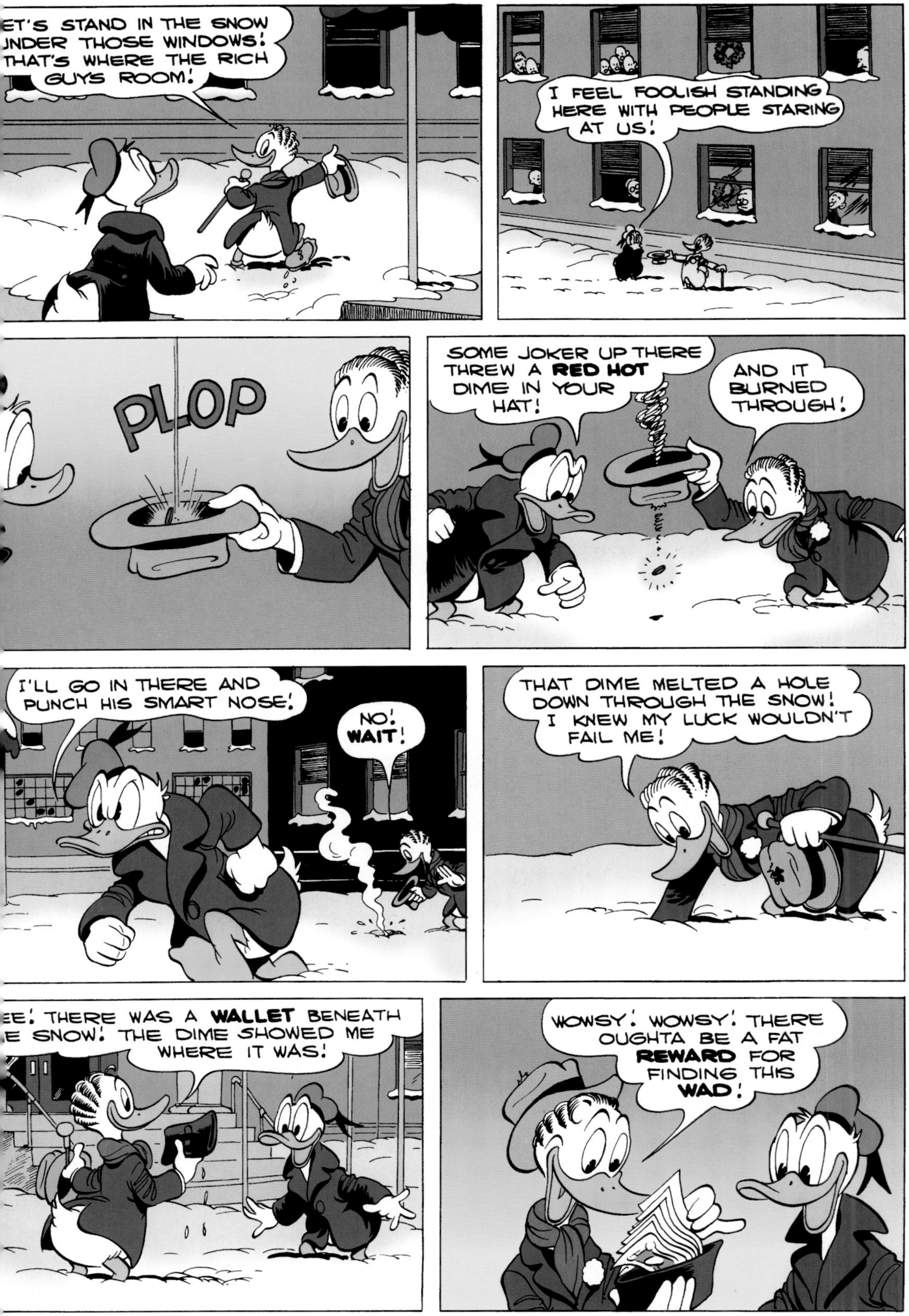

ET'S STAND IN THE SNOW UNDER THOSE WINDOWS! THAT'S WHERE THE RICH GUYS ROOM!
I FEEL FOOLISH STANDING HERE WITH PEOPLE STARING AT US!
PLOP
SOME JOKER UP THERE THREW A RED HOT DIME IN YOUR HAT!
AND IT BURNED THROUGH!
I'LL GO IN THERE AND PUNCH HIS SMART NOSE!
NO! WAIT!
THAT DIME MELTED A HOLE DOWN THROUGH THE SNOW! I KNEW MY LUCK WOULDN'T FAIL ME!
EE! THERE WAS A WALLET BENEATH E SNOW! THE DIME SHOWED ME WHERE IT WAS!
WOWSY! WOWSY! THERE OUGHTA BE A FAT REWARD FOR FINDING THIS WAD!

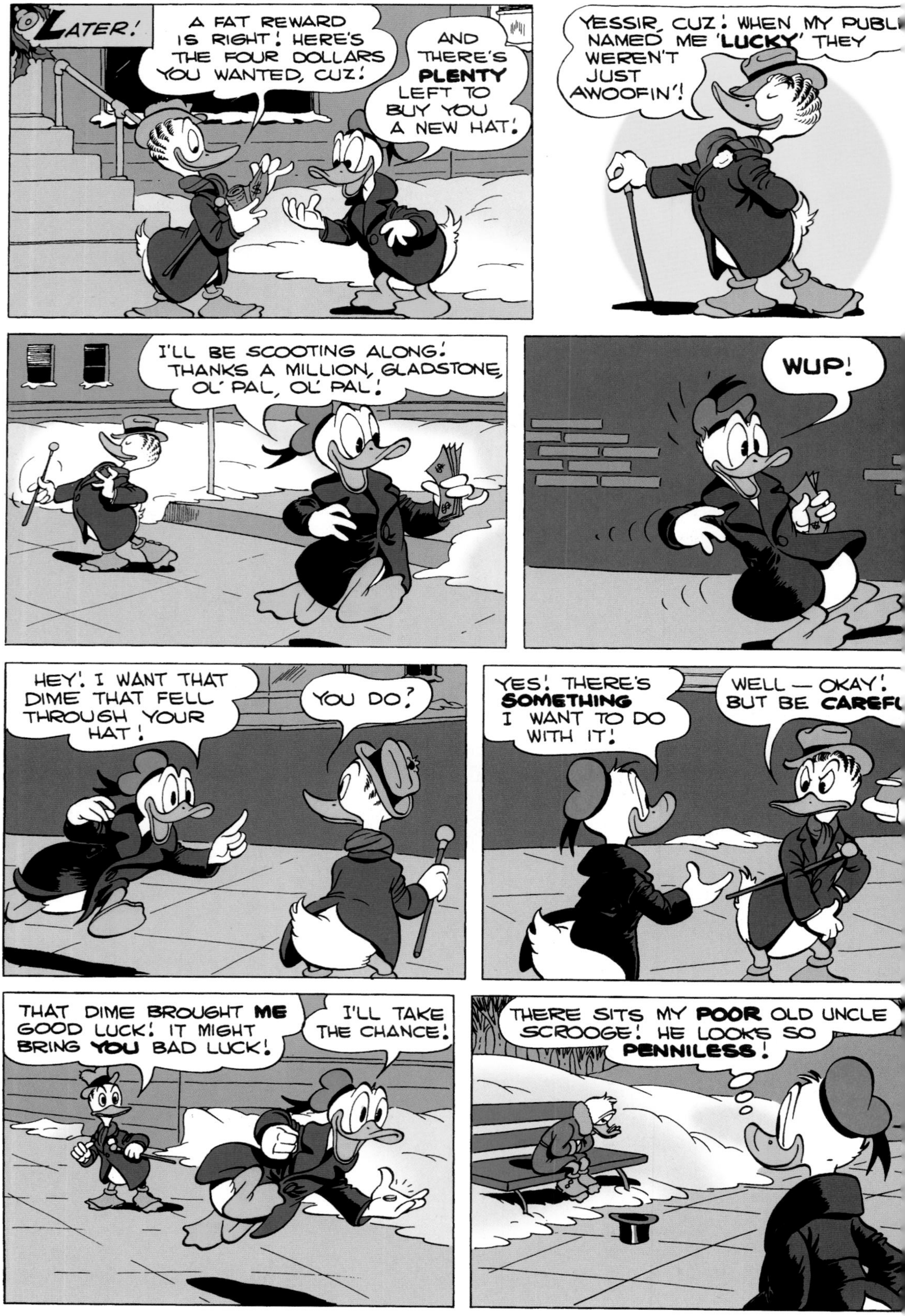
LATER!
A FAT REWARD IS RIGHT! HERE'S THE FOUR DOLLARS YOU WANTED, CUZ!
AND THERE'S **PLENTY** LEFT TO BUY YOU A NEW HAT!
YESSIR, CUZ! WHEN MY PUBL NAMED ME '**LUCKY**' THEY WEREN'T JUST AWOOFIN'!
I'LL BE SCOOTING ALONG! THANKS A MILLION, GLADSTONE, OL' PAL, OL' PAL!
WUP!
HEY! I WANT THAT DIME THAT FELL THROUGH YOUR HAT!
YOU DO?
YES! THERE'S **SOMETHING** I WANT TO DO WITH IT!
WELL — OKAY! BUT BE **CAREF**
THAT DIME BROUGHT **ME** GOOD LUCK! IT MIGHT BRING **YOU** BAD LUCK!
I'LL TAKE THE CHANCE!
THERE SITS MY **POOR** OLD UNCLE SCROOGE! HE LOOKS SO **PENNILESS**!

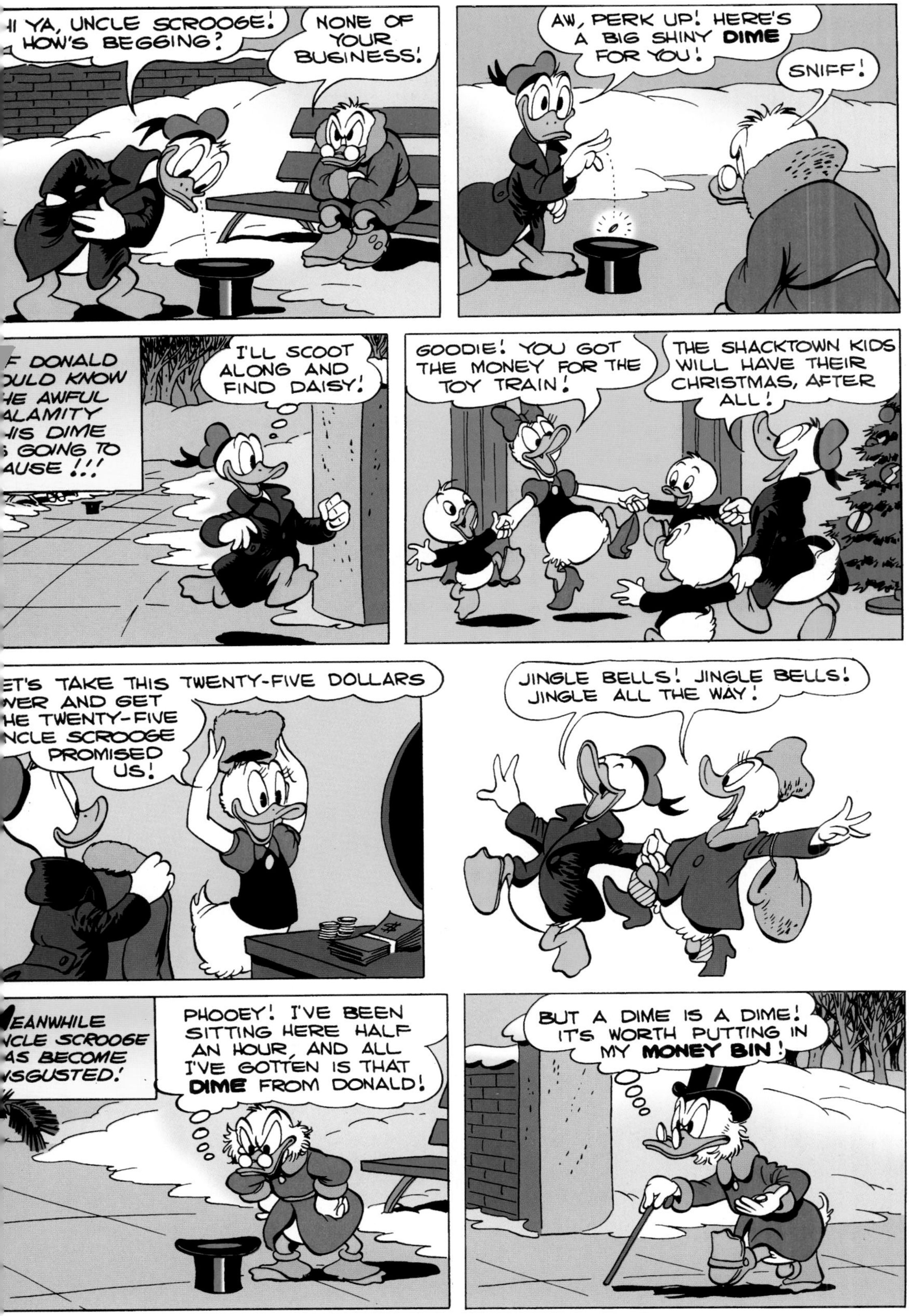

I YA, UNCLE SCROOGE! HOW'S BEGGING?
NONE OF YOUR BUSINESS!
AW, PERK UP! HERE'S A BIG SHINY DIME FOR YOU!
SNIFF!
F DONALD OULD KNOW HE AWFUL ALAMITY HIS DIME S GOING TO AUSE!!!
I'LL SCOOT ALONG AND FIND DAISY!
GOODIE! YOU GOT THE MONEY FOR THE TOY TRAIN!
THE SHACKTOWN KIDS WILL HAVE THEIR CHRISTMAS, AFTER ALL!
ET'S TAKE THIS TWENTY-FIVE DOLLARS WER AND GET HE TWENTY-FIVE NCLE SCROOGE PROMISED US!
JINGLE BELLS! JINGLE BELLS! JINGLE ALL THE WAY!
EANWHILE NCLE SCROOGE AS BECOME SGUSTED!
PHOOEY! I'VE BEEN SITTING HERE HALF AN HOUR, AND ALL I'VE GOTTEN IS THAT DIME FROM DONALD!
BUT A DIME IS A DIME! IT'S WORTH PUTTING IN MY MONEY BIN!

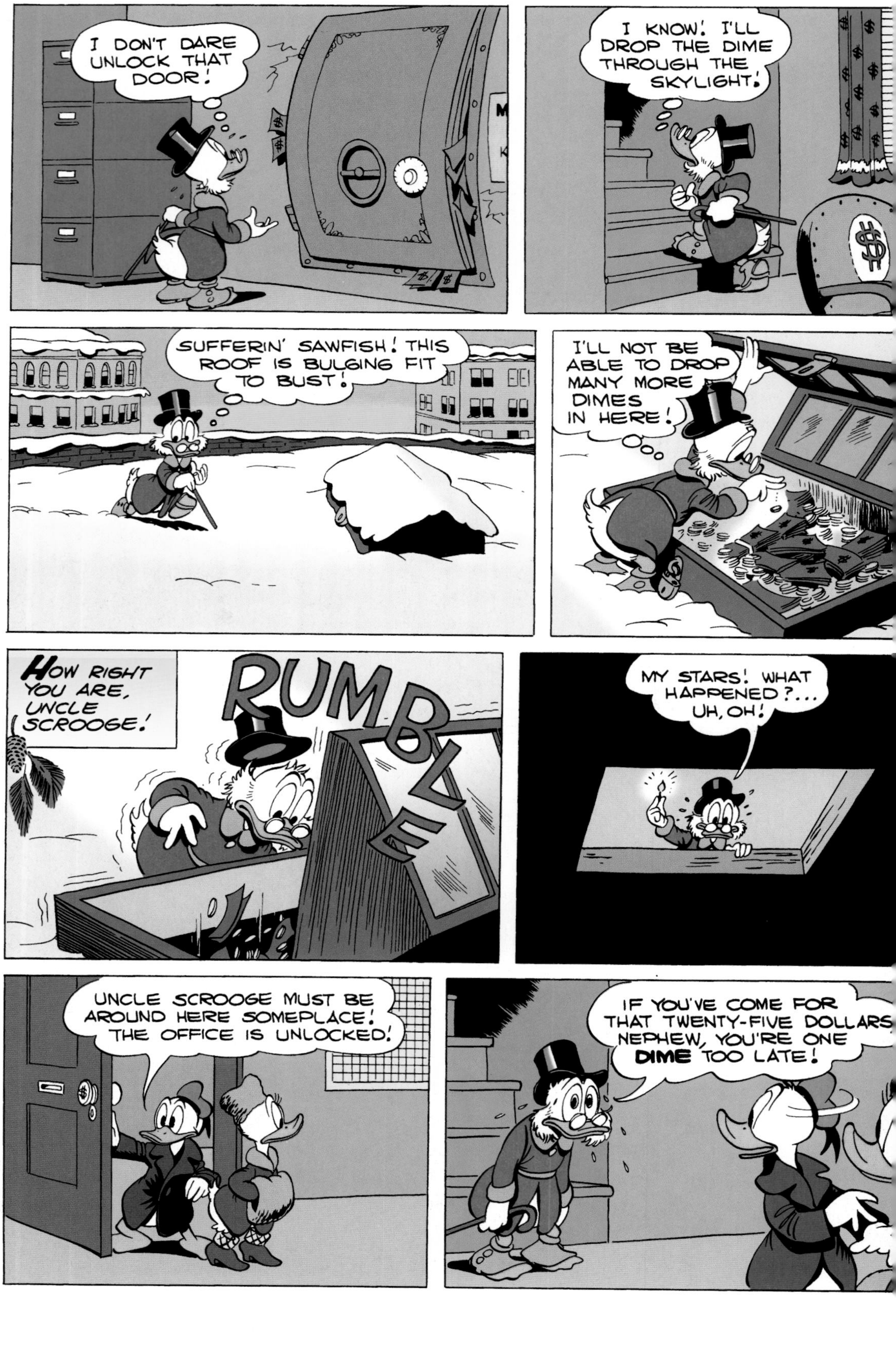
I DON'T DARE UNLOCK THAT DOOR!
I KNOW! I'LL DROP THE DIME THROUGH THE SKYLIGHT!
SUFFERIN' SAWFISH! THIS ROOF IS BULGING FIT TO BUST!
I'LL NOT BE ABLE TO DROP MANY MORE DIMES IN HERE!
HOW RIGHT YOU ARE, UNCLE SCROOGE!
RUMBLE
MY STARS! WHAT HAPPENED?... UH, OH!
UNCLE SCROOGE MUST BE AROUND HERE SOMEPLACE! THE OFFICE IS UNLOCKED!
IF YOU'VE COME FOR THAT TWENTY-FIVE DOLLARS, NEPHEW, YOU'RE ONE DIME TOO LATE!

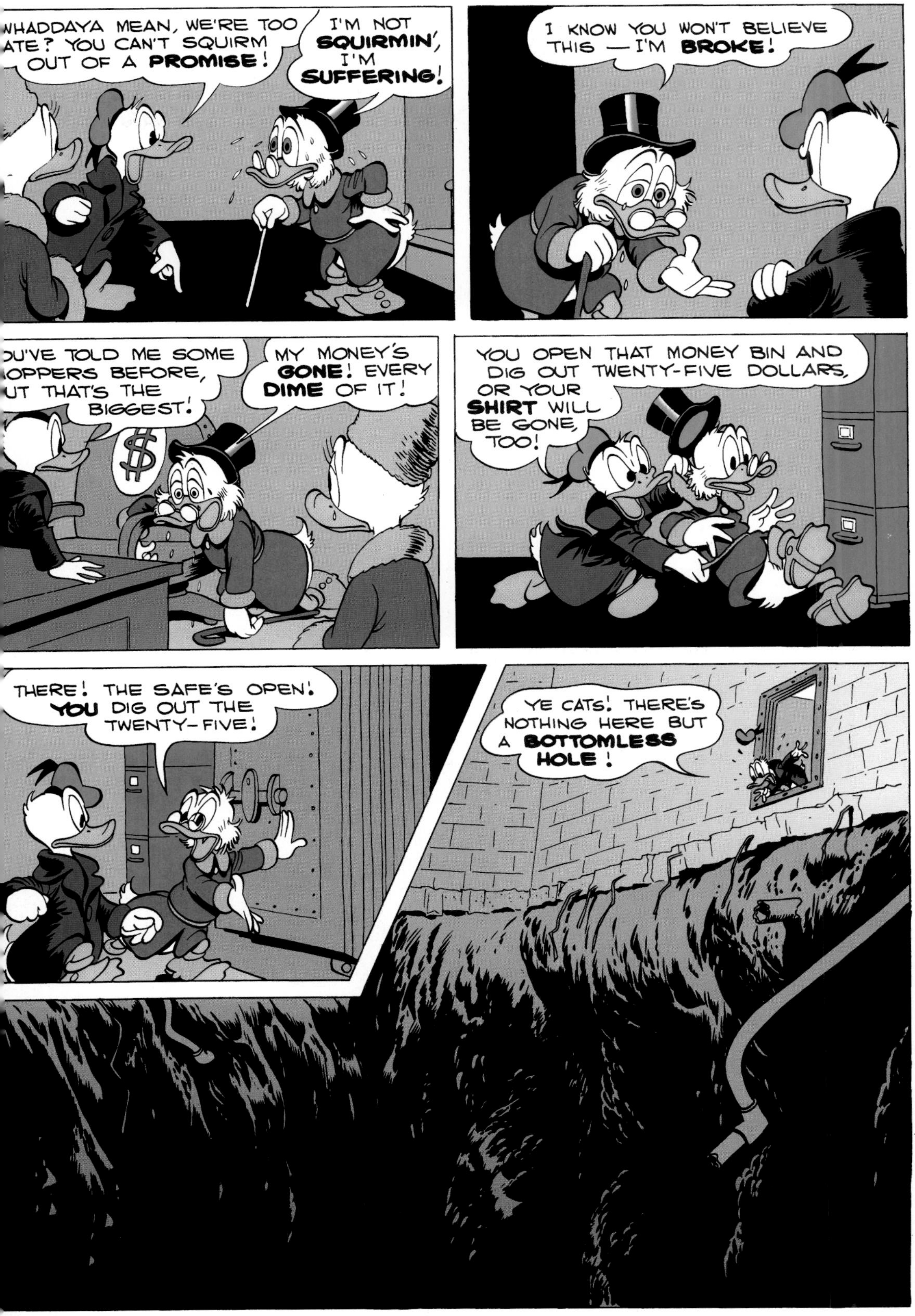
WHADDAYA MEAN, WE'RE TOO LATE? YOU CAN'T SQUIRM OUT OF A PROMISE!
I'M NOT SQUIRMIN', I'M SUFFERING!
I KNOW YOU WON'T BELIEVE THIS — I'M BROKE!
YOU'VE TOLD ME SOME WHOPPERS BEFORE, BUT THAT'S THE BIGGEST!
MY MONEY'S GONE! EVERY DIME OF IT!
$
YOU OPEN THAT MONEY BIN AND DIG OUT TWENTY-FIVE DOLLARS, OR YOUR SHIRT WILL BE GONE, TOO!
THERE! THE SAFE'S OPEN! YOU DIG OUT THE TWENTY-FIVE!
YE CATS! THERE'S NOTHING HERE BUT A BOTTOMLESS HOLE!

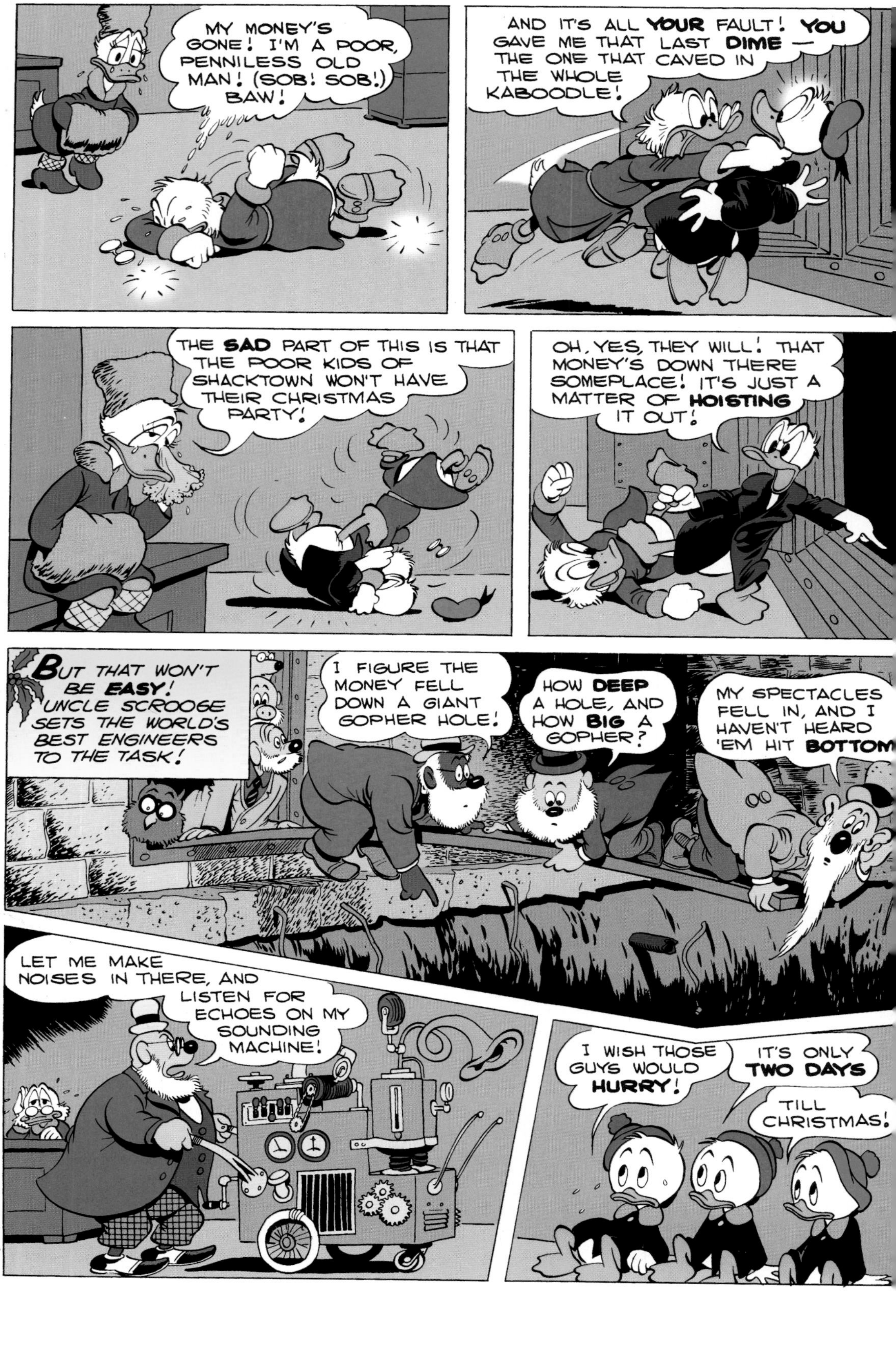
MY MONEY'S GONE! I'M A POOR, PENNILESS OLD MAN! (SOB! SOB!) BAW!
AND IT'S ALL YOUR FAULT! YOU GAVE ME THAT LAST DIME — THE ONE THAT CAVED IN THE WHOLE KABOODLE!
THE SAD PART OF THIS IS THAT THE POOR KIDS OF SHACKTOWN WON'T HAVE THEIR CHRISTMAS PARTY!
OH, YES, THEY WILL! THAT MONEY'S DOWN THERE SOMEPLACE! IT'S JUST A MATTER OF HOISTING IT OUT!
BUT THAT WON'T BE EASY! UNCLE SCROOGE SETS THE WORLD'S BEST ENGINEERS TO THE TASK!
I FIGURE THE MONEY FELL DOWN A GIANT GOPHER HOLE!
HOW DEEP A HOLE, AND HOW BIG A GOPHER?
MY SPECTACLES FELL IN, AND I HAVEN'T HEARD 'EM HIT BOTTOM
LET ME MAKE NOISES IN THERE, AND LISTEN FOR ECHOES ON MY SOUNDING MACHINE!
I WISH THOSE GUYS WOULD HURRY!
IT'S ONLY TWO DAYS
TILL CHRISTMAS!

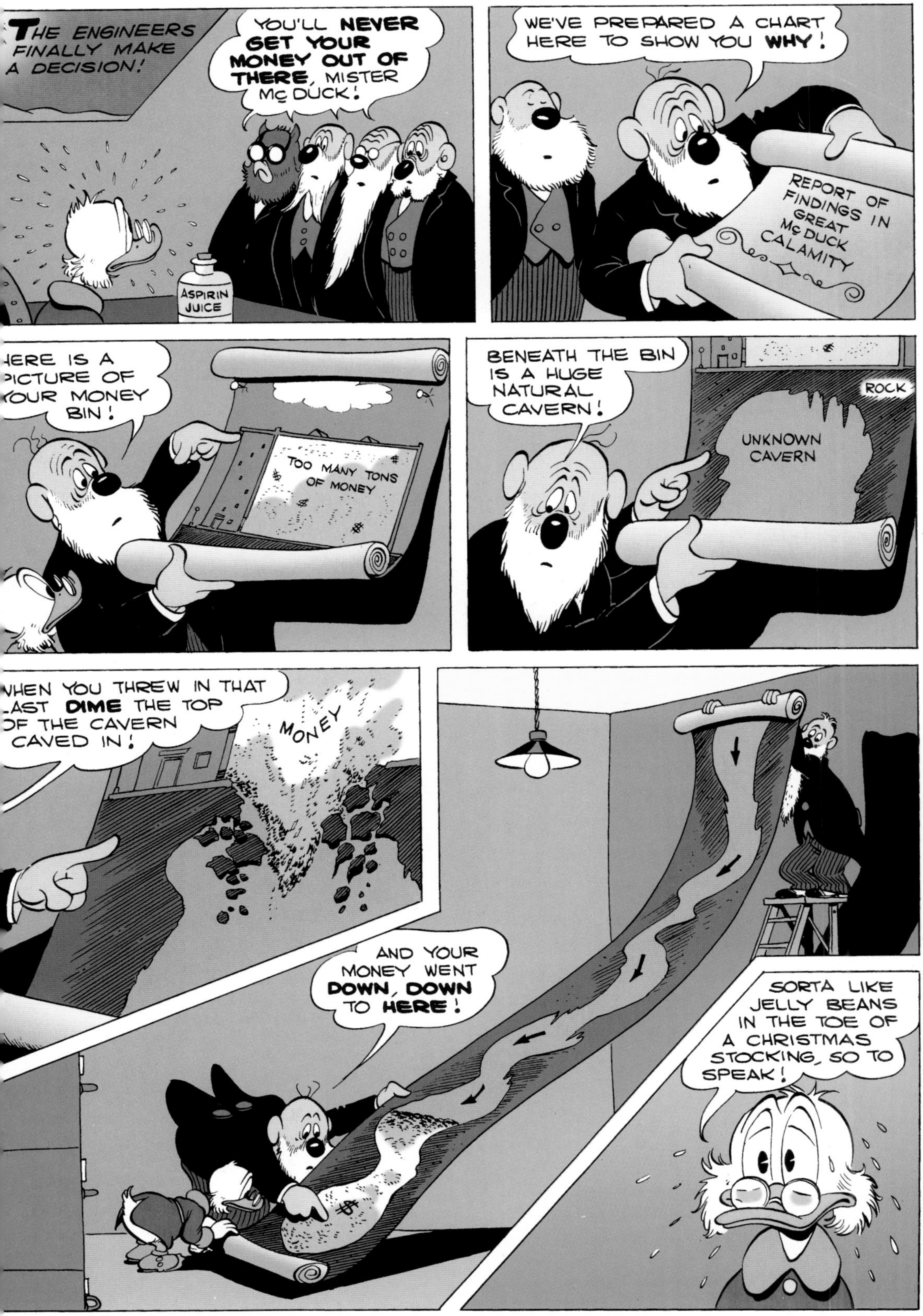
THE ENGINEERS FINALLY MAKE A DECISION!
YOU'LL NEVER GET YOUR MONEY OUT OF THERE, MISTER MC DUCK!
ASPIRIN JUICE
WE'VE PREPARED A CHART HERE TO SHOW YOU WHY!
REPORT OF FINDINGS IN GREAT MC DUCK CALAMITY
HERE IS A PICTURE OF YOUR MONEY BIN!
TOO MANY TONS OF MONEY
BENEATH THE BIN IS A HUGE NATURAL CAVERN!
ROCK
UNKNOWN CAVERN
WHEN YOU THREW IN THAT LAST DIME THE TOP OF THE CAVERN CAVED IN!
MONEY
AND YOUR MONEY WENT DOWN, DOWN TO HERE!
SORTA LIKE JELLY BEANS IN THE TOE OF A CHRISTMAS STOCKING, SO TO SPEAK!

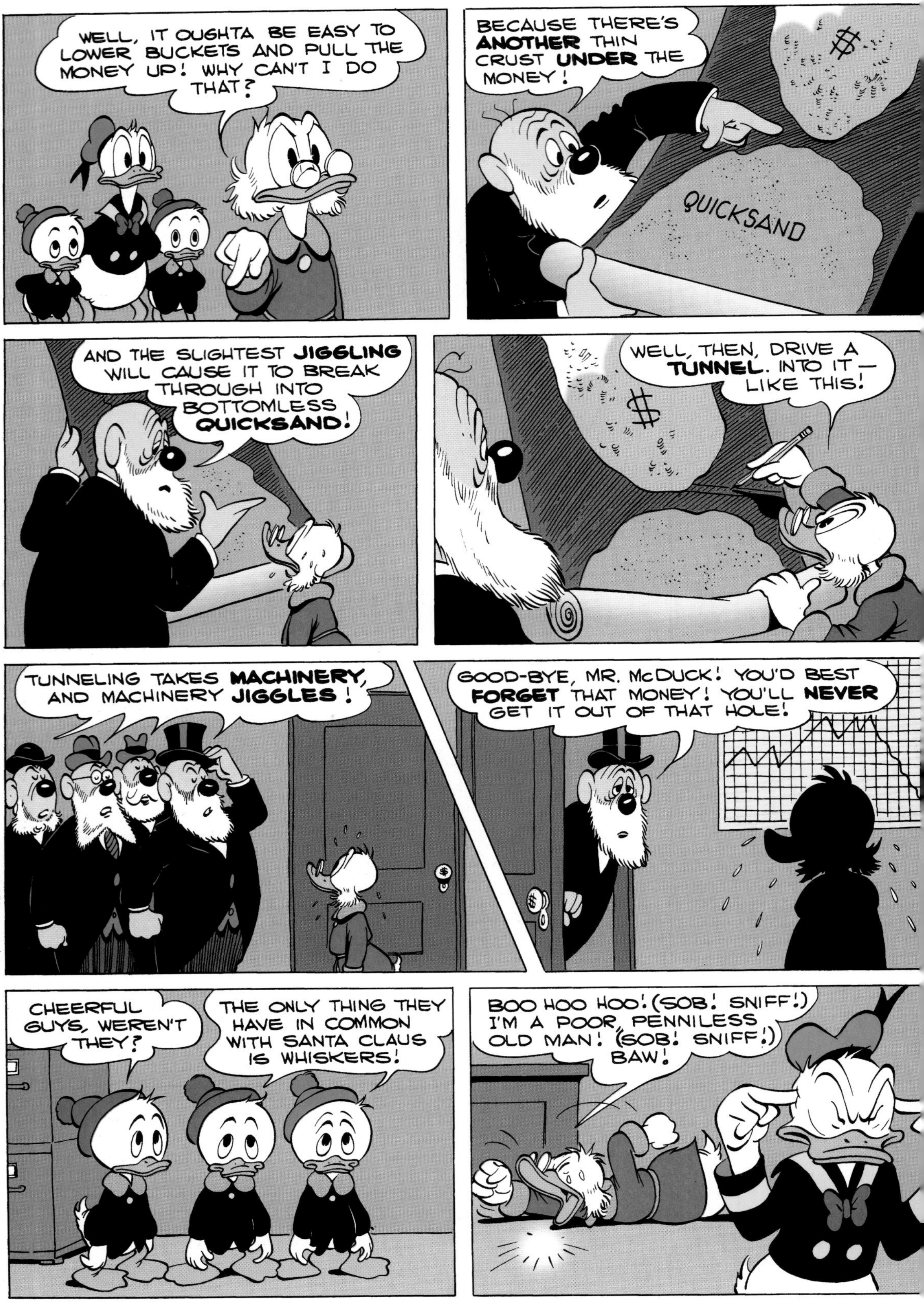
WELL, IT OUGHTA BE EASY TO LOWER BUCKETS AND PULL THE MONEY UP! WHY CAN'T I DO THAT?
BECAUSE THERE'S ANOTHER THIN CRUST UNDER THE MONEY!
QUICKSAND
AND THE SLIGHTEST JIGGLING WILL CAUSE IT TO BREAK THROUGH INTO BOTTOMLESS QUICKSAND!
WELL, THEN, DRIVE A TUNNEL INTO IT — LIKE THIS!
TUNNELING TAKES MACHINERY, AND MACHINERY JIGGLES!
GOOD-BYE, MR. McDUCK! YOU'D BEST FORGET THAT MONEY! YOU'LL NEVER GET IT OUT OF THAT HOLE!
CHEERFUL GUYS, WEREN'T THEY?
THE ONLY THING THEY HAVE IN COMMON WITH SANTA CLAUS IS WHISKERS!
BOO HOO HOO! (SOB! SNIFF!) I'M A POOR, PENNILESS OLD MAN! (SOB! SNIFF!) BAW!

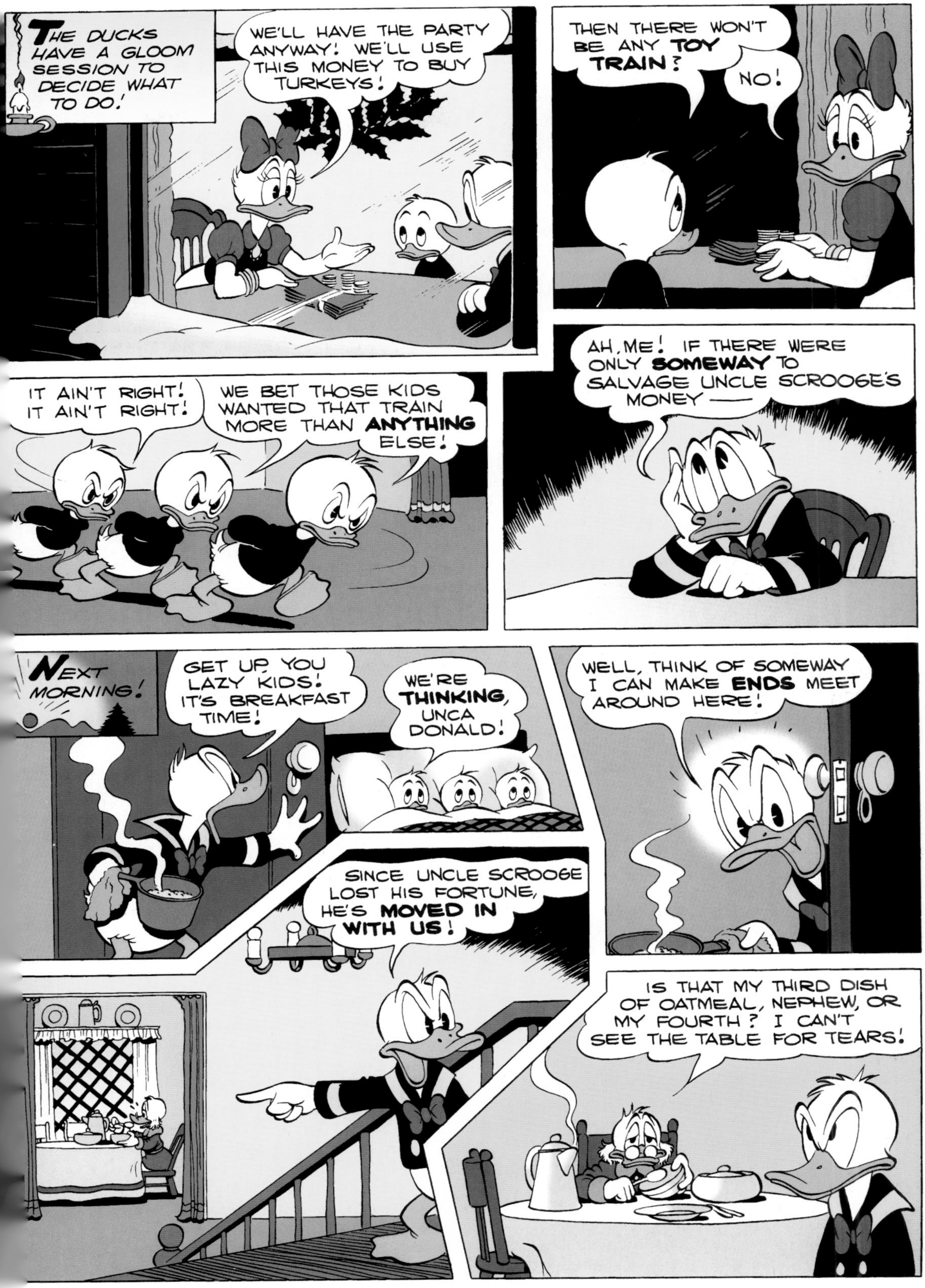
THE DUCKS HAVE A GLOOM SESSION TO DECIDE WHAT TO DO!
WE'LL HAVE THE PARTY ANYWAY! WE'LL USE THIS MONEY TO BUY TURKEYS!
THEN THERE WON'T BE ANY TOY TRAIN?
NO!
IT AIN'T RIGHT! IT AIN'T RIGHT!
WE BET THOSE KIDS WANTED THAT TRAIN MORE THAN ANYTHING ELSE!
AH, ME! IF THERE WERE ONLY SOMEWAY TO SALVAGE UNCLE SCROOGE'S MONEY ——
NEXT MORNING!
GET UP, YOU LAZY KIDS! IT'S BREAKFAST TIME!
WE'RE THINKING, UNCA DONALD!
WELL, THINK OF SOMEWAY I CAN MAKE ENDS MEET AROUND HERE!
SINCE UNCLE SCROOGE LOST HIS FORTUNE, HE'S MOVED IN WITH US!
IS THAT MY THIRD DISH OF OATMEAL, NEPHEW, OR MY FOURTH? I CAN'T SEE THE TABLE FOR TEARS!

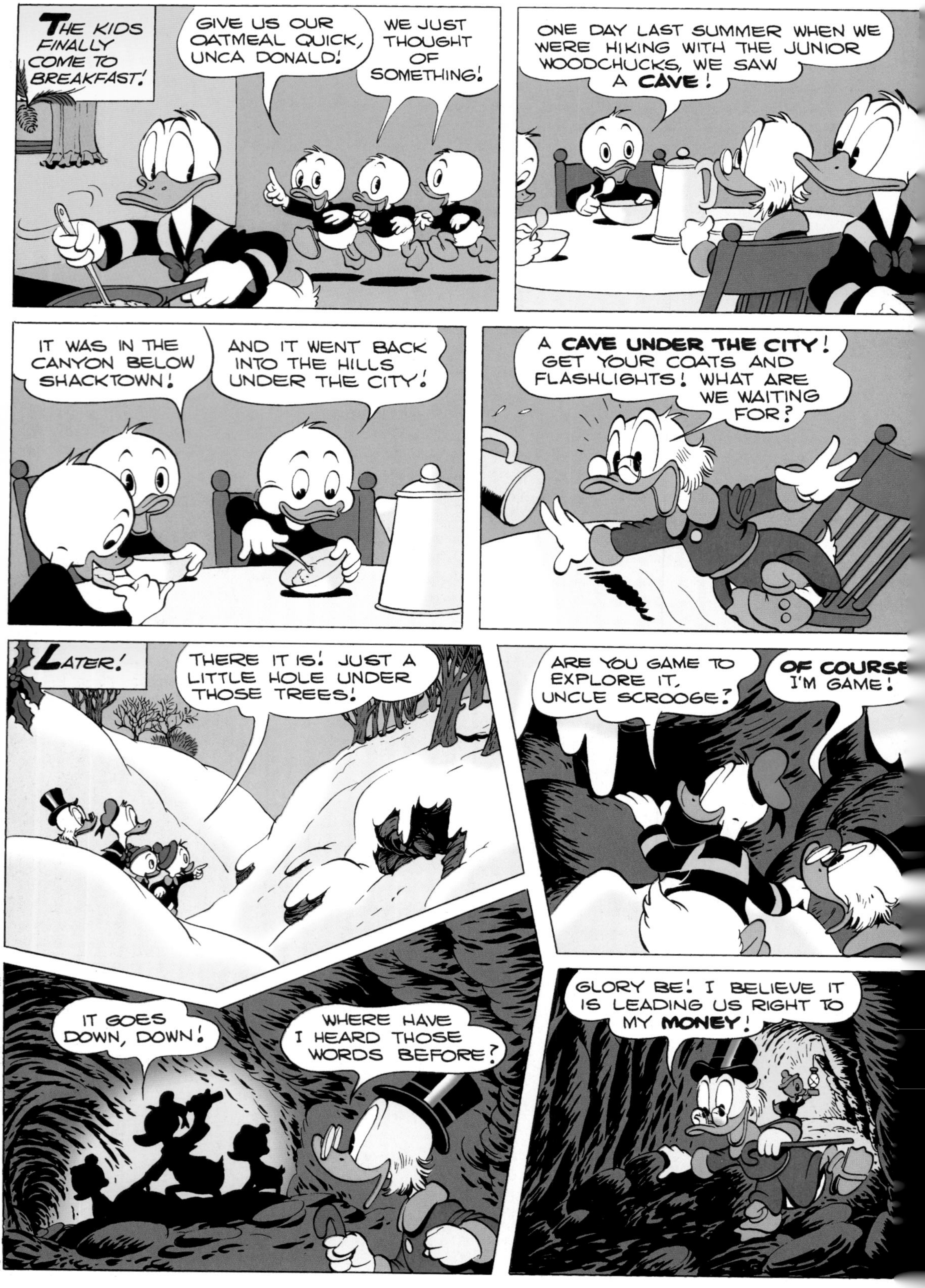
THE KIDS FINALLY COME TO BREAKFAST!
GIVE US OUR OATMEAL QUICK, UNCA DONALD!
WE JUST THOUGHT OF SOMETHING!
ONE DAY LAST SUMMER WHEN WE WERE HIKING WITH THE JUNIOR WOODCHUCKS, WE SAW A CAVE!
IT WAS IN THE CANYON BELOW SHACKTOWN!
AND IT WENT BACK INTO THE HILLS UNDER THE CITY!
A CAVE UNDER THE CITY! GET YOUR COATS AND FLASHLIGHTS! WHAT ARE WE WAITING FOR?
LATER!
THERE IT IS! JUST A LITTLE HOLE UNDER THOSE TREES!
ARE YOU GAME TO EXPLORE IT, UNCLE SCROOGE?
OF COURSE I'M GAME!
IT GOES DOWN, DOWN!
WHERE HAVE I HEARD THOSE WORDS BEFORE?
GLORY BE! I BELIEVE IT IS LEADING US RIGHT TO MY MONEY!

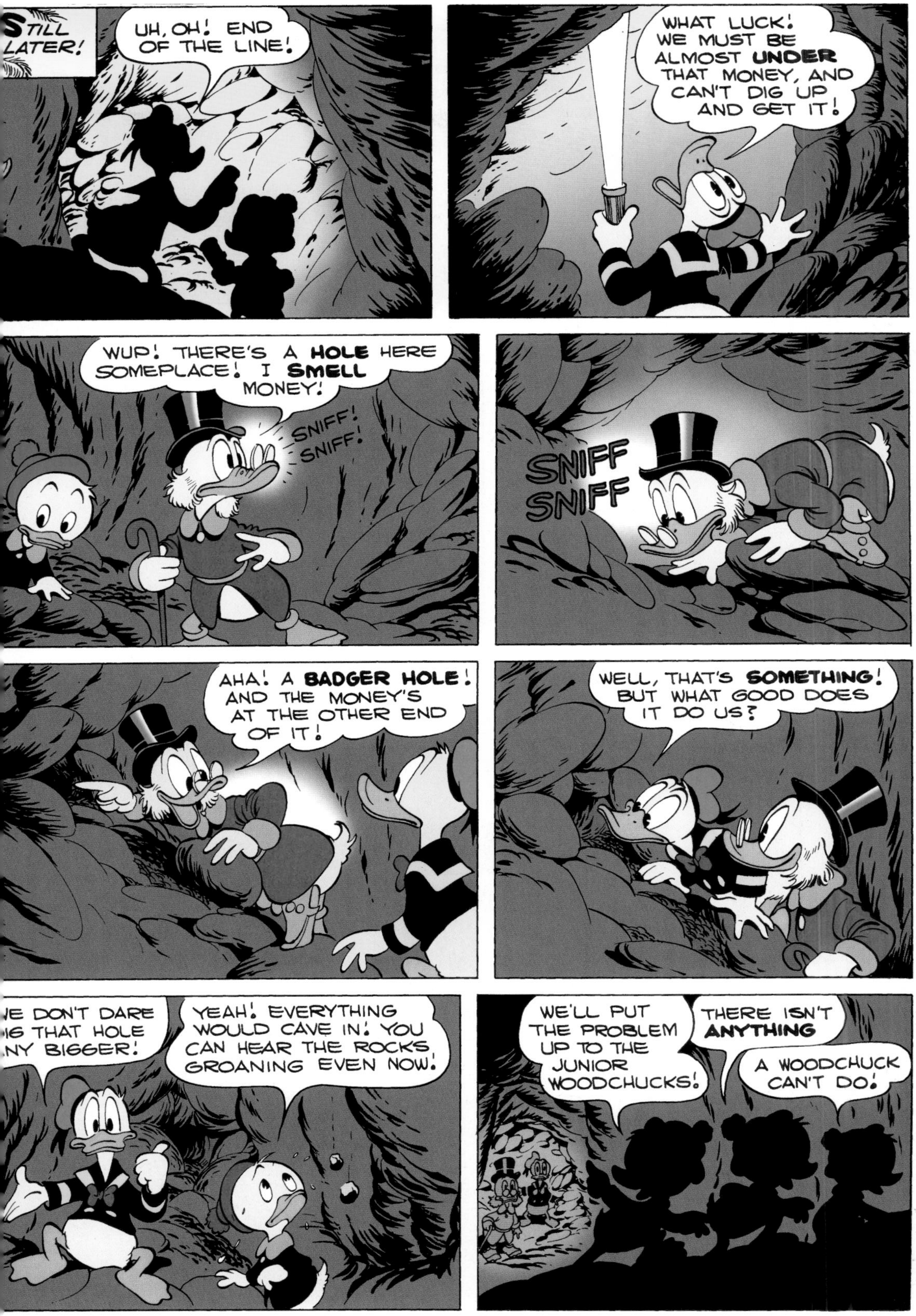
STILL LATER!
UH, OH! END OF THE LINE!
WHAT LUCK! WE MUST BE ALMOST UNDER THAT MONEY, AND CAN'T DIG UP AND GET IT!
WUP! THERE'S A HOLE HERE SOMEPLACE! I SMELL MONEY!
SNIFF! SNIFF!
SNIFF SNIFF
AHA! A BADGER HOLE! AND THE MONEY'S AT THE OTHER END OF IT!
WELL, THAT'S SOMETHING! BUT WHAT GOOD DOES IT DO US?
WE DON'T DARE DIG THAT HOLE ANY BIGGER!
YEAH! EVERYTHING WOULD CAVE IN! YOU CAN HEAR THE ROCKS GROANING EVEN NOW!
WE'LL PUT THE PROBLEM UP TO THE JUNIOR WOODCHUCKS!
THERE ISN'T ANYTHING
A WOODCHUCK CAN'T DO!

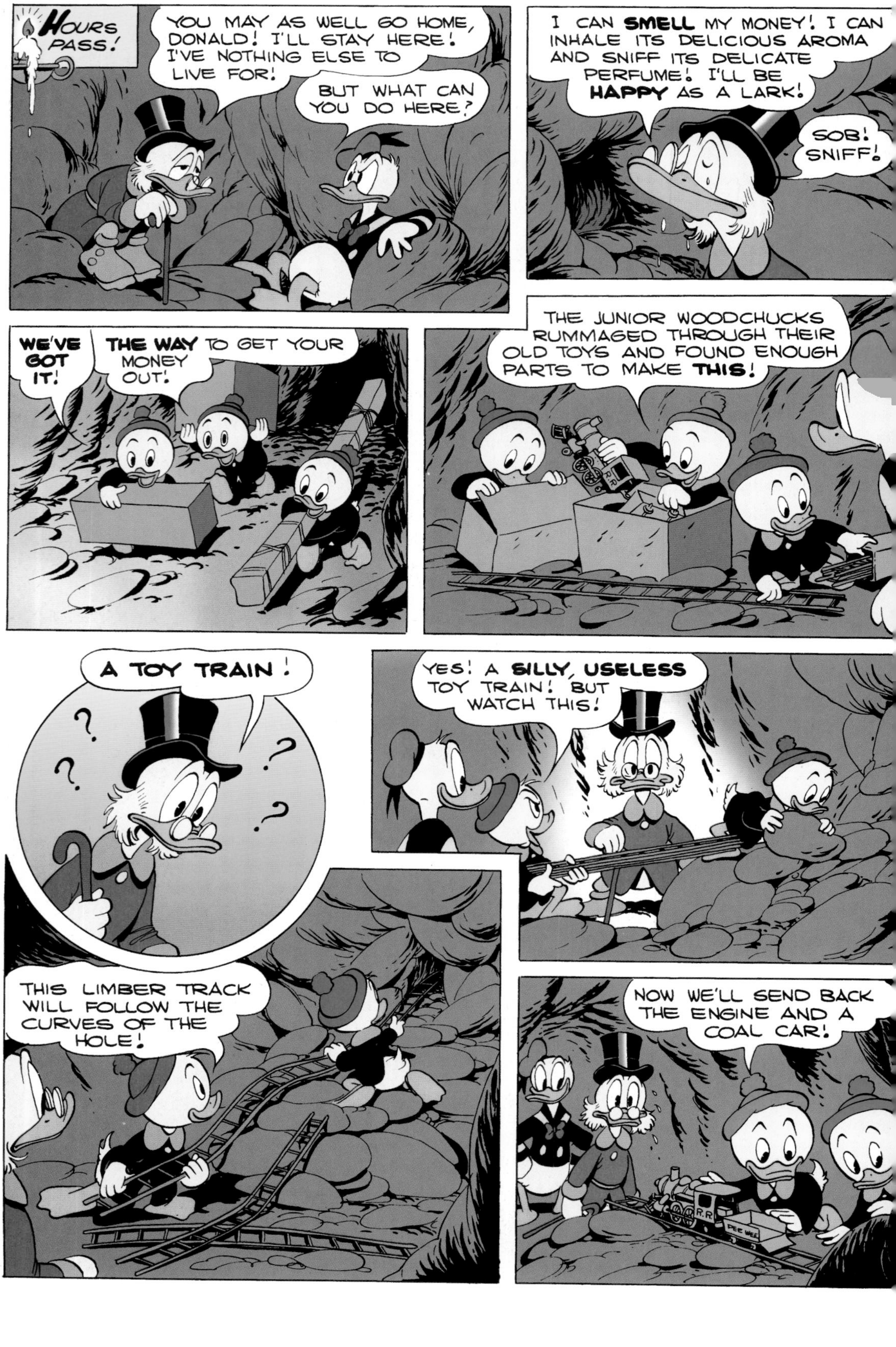
HOURS PASS!
YOU MAY AS WELL GO HOME, DONALD! I'LL STAY HERE! I'VE NOTHING ELSE TO LIVE FOR!
BUT WHAT CAN YOU DO HERE?
I CAN SMELL MY MONEY! I CAN INHALE ITS DELICIOUS AROMA AND SNIFF ITS DELICATE PERFUME! I'LL BE HAPPY AS A LARK!
SOB! SNIFF!
WE'VE GOT IT!
THE WAY TO GET YOUR MONEY OUT!
THE JUNIOR WOODCHUCKS RUMMAGED THROUGH THEIR OLD TOYS AND FOUND ENOUGH PARTS TO MAKE THIS!
A TOY TRAIN!
YES! A SILLY, USELESS TOY TRAIN! BUT WATCH THIS!
THIS LIMBER TRACK WILL FOLLOW THE CURVES OF THE HOLE!
NOW WE'LL SEND BACK THE ENGINE AND A COAL CAR!

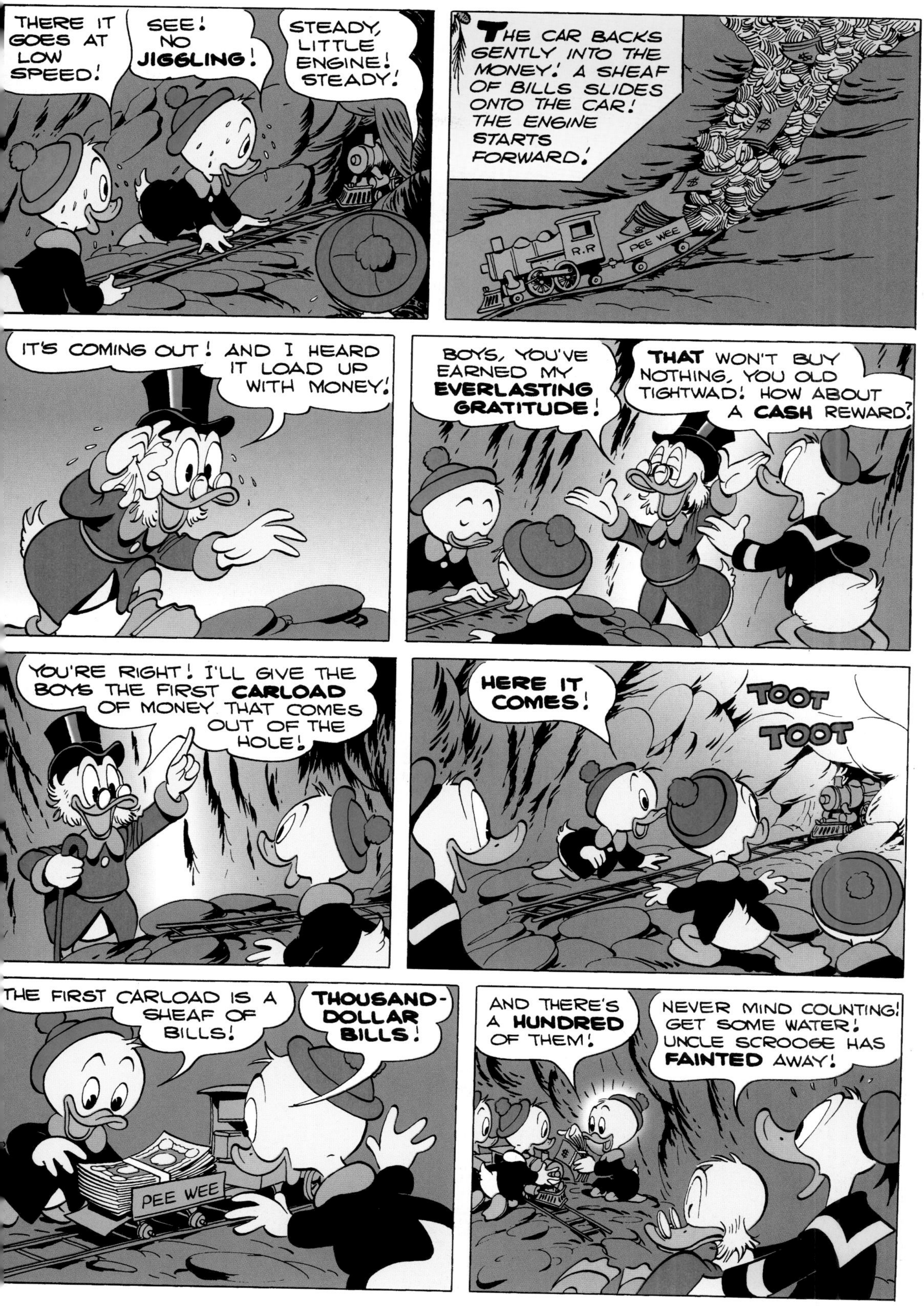
THERE IT GOES AT LOW SPEED!
SEE! NO JIGGLING!
STEADY, LITTLE ENGINE! STEADY!
THE CAR BACKS GENTLY INTO THE MONEY! A SHEAF OF BILLS SLIDES ONTO THE CAR! THE ENGINE STARTS FORWARD!
R.R
PEE WEE
IT'S COMING OUT! AND I HEARD IT LOAD UP WITH MONEY!
BOYS, YOU'VE EARNED MY EVERLASTING GRATITUDE!
THAT WON'T BUY NOTHING, YOU OLD TIGHTWAD! HOW ABOUT A CASH REWARD?
YOU'RE RIGHT! I'LL GIVE THE BOYS THE FIRST CARLOAD OF MONEY THAT COMES OUT OF THE HOLE!
HERE IT COMES!
TOOT
TOOT
THE FIRST CARLOAD IS A SHEAF OF BILLS!
THOUSAND-DOLLAR BILLS!
PEE WEE
AND THERE'S A HUNDRED OF THEM!
NEVER MIND COUNTING! GET SOME WATER! UNCLE SCROOGE HAS FAINTED AWAY!

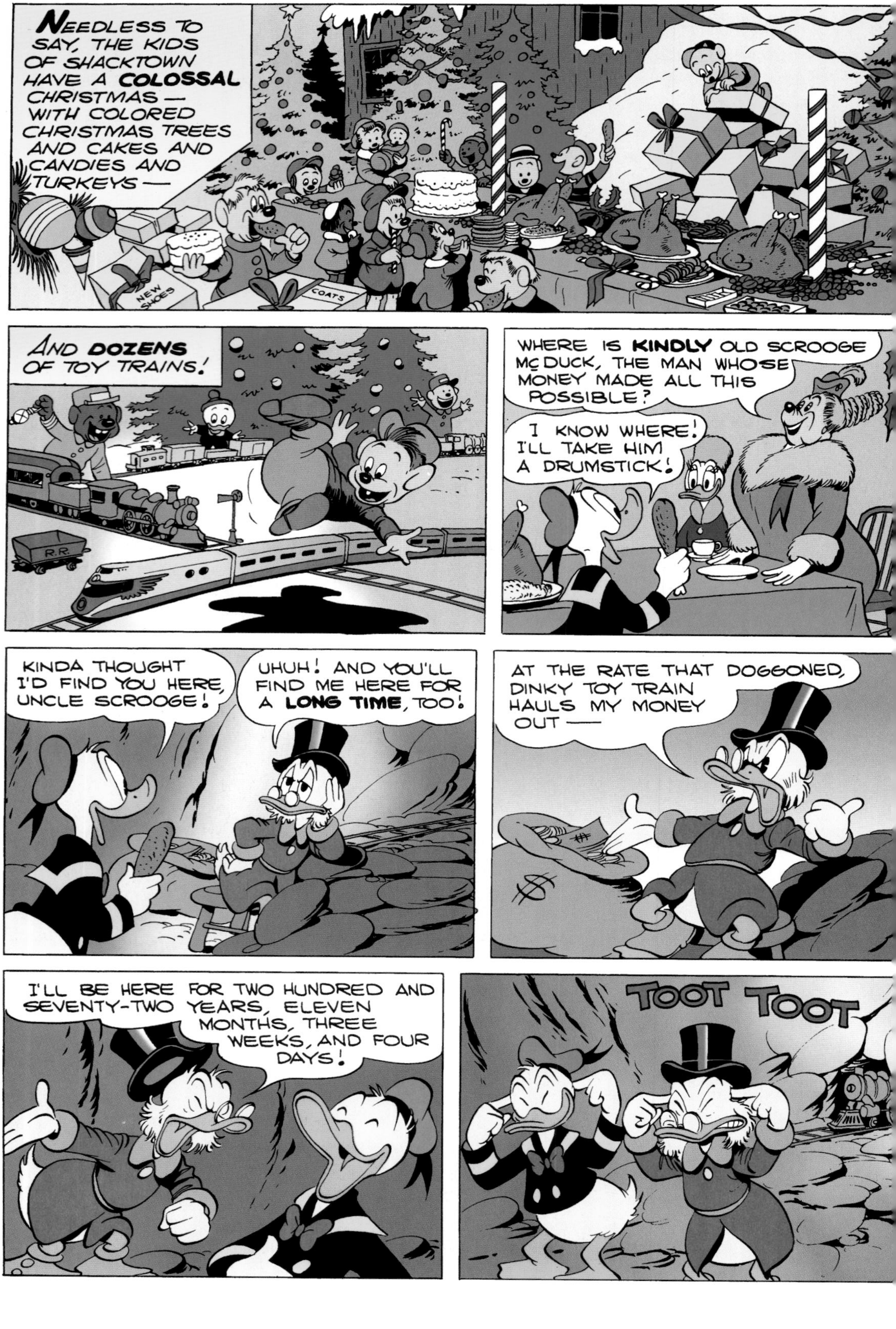
NEEDLESS TO SAY, THE KIDS OF SHACKTOWN HAVE A **COLOSSAL** CHRISTMAS — WITH COLORED CHRISTMAS TREES AND CAKES AND CANDIES AND TURKEYS —
NEW SHOES
COATS
AND **DOZENS** OF TOY TRAINS!
R.R.
WHERE IS **KINDLY** OLD SCROOGE McDUCK, THE MAN WHOSE MONEY MADE ALL THIS POSSIBLE?
I KNOW WHERE! I'LL TAKE HIM A DRUMSTICK!
KINDA THOUGHT I'D FIND YOU HERE, UNCLE SCROOGE!
UHUH! AND YOU'LL FIND ME HERE FOR A **LONG TIME**, TOO!
AT THE RATE THAT DOGGONED, DINKY TOY TRAIN HAULS MY MONEY OUT —
I'LL BE HERE FOR TWO HUNDRED AND SEVENTY-TWO YEARS, ELEVEN MONTHS, THREE WEEKS, AND FOUR DAYS!
TOOT TOOT

THE DUCK AND THE MOUSE SENT TO YOUR HOUSE!

©2004 Disney Enterprises, Inc.

Whether it's Uncle Scrooge or Donald, Mickey or Minnie, subscribe now and all the fun in the months to come from Gemstone Publishing's exciting line of Disney comic books will arrive at your doorstep.

For collectors: Walt Disney's Comics and Stories and Uncle Scrooge, providing the best of vintage and recent classic tales by such highly-acclaimed creators as Carl Barks, Pat Block, Daniel Branca, Cesar Ferioli, David Gerstein, Michael T. Gilbert, Daan Jippes, Don Markstein, Pat McGreal, Dave Rawson, Don Rosa, Noel Van Horn, William Van Horn, and many more. These books are 64 pages and in the sturdy, squarebound prestige format that collectors love.

For readers on the go: Donald Duck Adventures, our 5" X 7½" "Take-Along Comic" series, gives you long adventure stories starring Mickey, Donald, Scrooge, and others in modern stories that take them beyond the limits of space and time.

For readers of all ages: Donald Duck and Mickey Mouse and Friends, offering Disney fans the best contemporary Mouse and Duck stories in the familiar 32-page, stapled, comic book format.

Look for them at your local comic shop! Can't find a comic shop? Try the Toll Free Comic Shop Locator Service at (888) COMIC BOOK for the shop nearest you! If you can't find Gemstone's Disney comics in your neighborhood you may subscribe at no extra charge, and we'll pay the postage! Use the coupon below, or a copy!

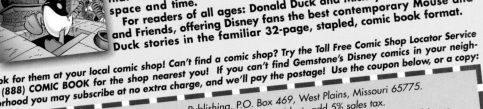

www.gemstonepub.com

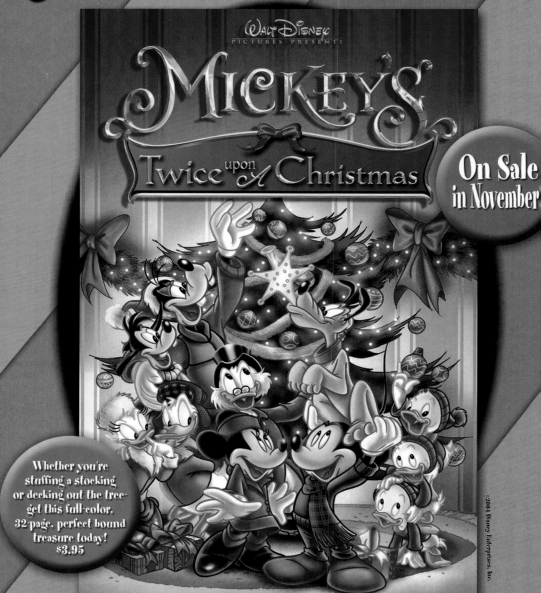

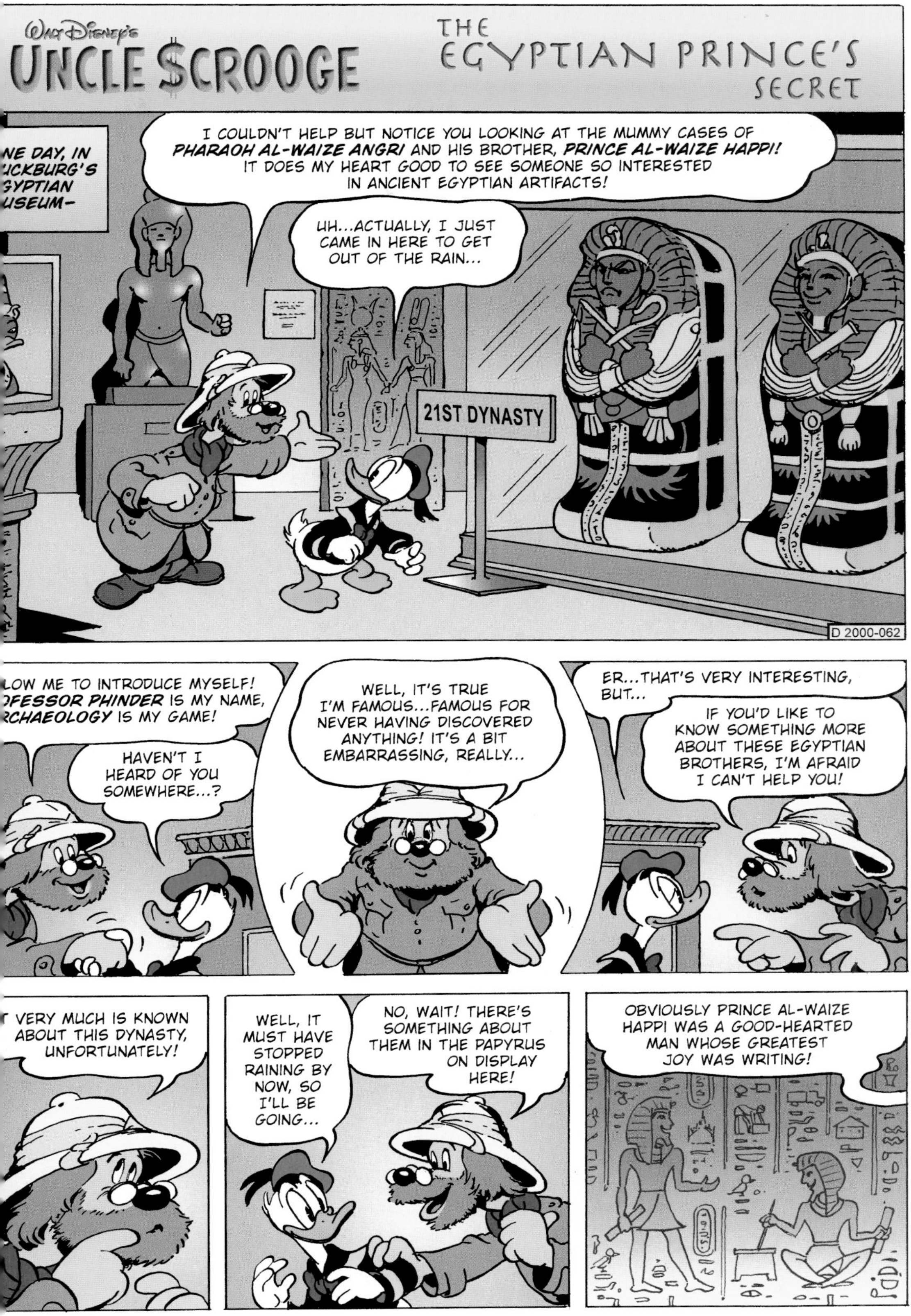

WALT DISNEY'S UNCLE $CROOGE
THE EGYPTIAN PRINCE'S SECRET
NE DAY, IN UCKBURG'S GYPTIAN USEUM—
I COULDN'T HELP BUT NOTICE YOU LOOKING AT THE MUMMY CASES OF PHARAOH AL-WAIZE ANGRI AND HIS BROTHER, PRINCE AL-WAIZE HAPPI! IT DOES MY HEART GOOD TO SEE SOMEONE SO INTERESTED IN ANCIENT EGYPTIAN ARTIFACTS!
UH...ACTUALLY, I JUST CAME IN HERE TO GET OUT OF THE RAIN...
21ST DYNASTY
D 2000-062
LOW ME TO INTRODUCE MYSELF! OFESSOR PHINDER IS MY NAME, RCHAEOLOGY IS MY GAME!
HAVEN'T I HEARD OF YOU SOMEWHERE...?
WELL, IT'S TRUE I'M FAMOUS...FAMOUS FOR NEVER HAVING DISCOVERED ANYTHING! IT'S A BIT EMBARRASSING, REALLY...
ER...THAT'S VERY INTERESTING, BUT...
IF YOU'D LIKE TO KNOW SOMETHING MORE ABOUT THESE EGYPTIAN BROTHERS, I'M AFRAID I CAN'T HELP YOU!
T VERY MUCH IS KNOWN ABOUT THIS DYNASTY, UNFORTUNATELY!
WELL, IT MUST HAVE STOPPED RAINING BY NOW, SO I'LL BE GOING...
NO, WAIT! THERE'S SOMETHING ABOUT THEM IN THE PAPYRUS ON DISPLAY HERE!
OBVIOUSLY PRINCE AL-WAIZE HAPPI WAS A GOOD-HEARTED MAN WHOSE GREATEST JOY WAS WRITING!

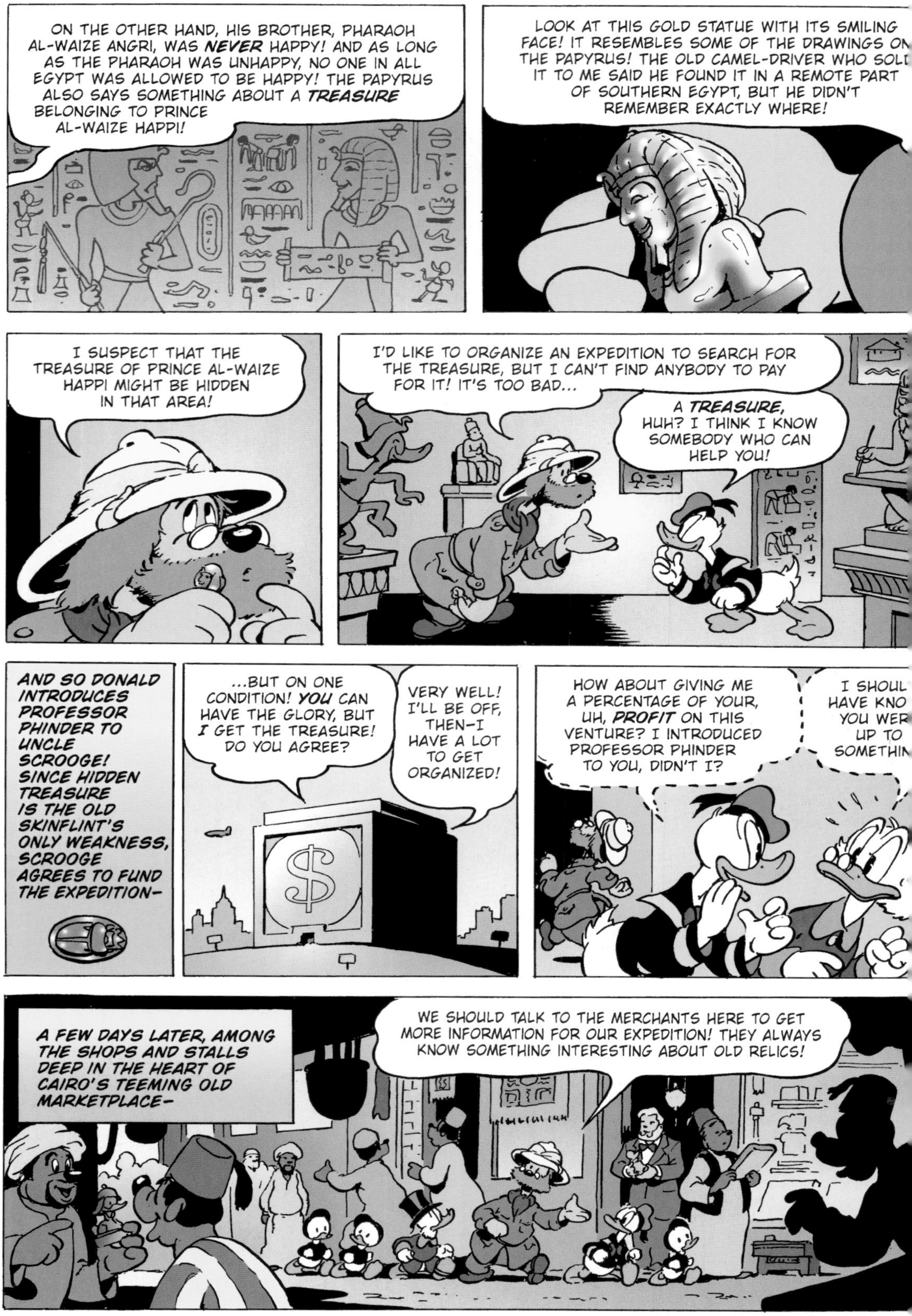

ON THE OTHER HAND, HIS BROTHER, PHARAOH AL-WAIZE ANGRI, WAS NEVER HAPPY! AND AS LONG AS THE PHARAOH WAS UNHAPPY, NO ONE IN ALL EGYPT WAS ALLOWED TO BE HAPPY! THE PAPYRUS ALSO SAYS SOMETHING ABOUT A TREASURE BELONGING TO PRINCE AL-WAIZE HAPPI!
LOOK AT THIS GOLD STATUE WITH ITS SMILING FACE! IT RESEMBLES SOME OF THE DRAWINGS ON THE PAPYRUS! THE OLD CAMEL-DRIVER WHO SOLD IT TO ME SAID HE FOUND IT IN A REMOTE PART OF SOUTHERN EGYPT, BUT HE DIDN'T REMEMBER EXACTLY WHERE!
I SUSPECT THAT THE TREASURE OF PRINCE AL-WAIZE HAPPI MIGHT BE HIDDEN IN THAT AREA!
I'D LIKE TO ORGANIZE AN EXPEDITION TO SEARCH FOR THE TREASURE, BUT I CAN'T FIND ANYBODY TO PAY FOR IT! IT'S TOO BAD...
A TREASURE, HUH? I THINK I KNOW SOMEBODY WHO CAN HELP YOU!
AND SO DONALD INTRODUCES PROFESSOR PHINDER TO UNCLE SCROOGE! SINCE HIDDEN TREASURE IS THE OLD SKINFLINT'S ONLY WEAKNESS, SCROOGE AGREES TO FUND THE EXPEDITION–
...BUT ON ONE CONDITION! YOU CAN HAVE THE GLORY, BUT I GET THE TREASURE! DO YOU AGREE?
VERY WELL! I'LL BE OFF, THEN–I HAVE A LOT TO GET ORGANIZED!
HOW ABOUT GIVING ME A PERCENTAGE OF YOUR, UH, PROFIT ON THIS VENTURE? I INTRODUCED PROFESSOR PHINDER TO YOU, DIDN'T I?
I SHOUL HAVE KNO YOU WER UP TO SOMETHIN
A FEW DAYS LATER, AMONG THE SHOPS AND STALLS DEEP IN THE HEART OF CAIRO'S TEEMING OLD MARKETPLACE–
WE SHOULD TALK TO THE MERCHANTS HERE TO GET MORE INFORMATION FOR OUR EXPEDITION! THEY ALWAYS KNOW SOMETHING INTERESTING ABOUT OLD RELICS!

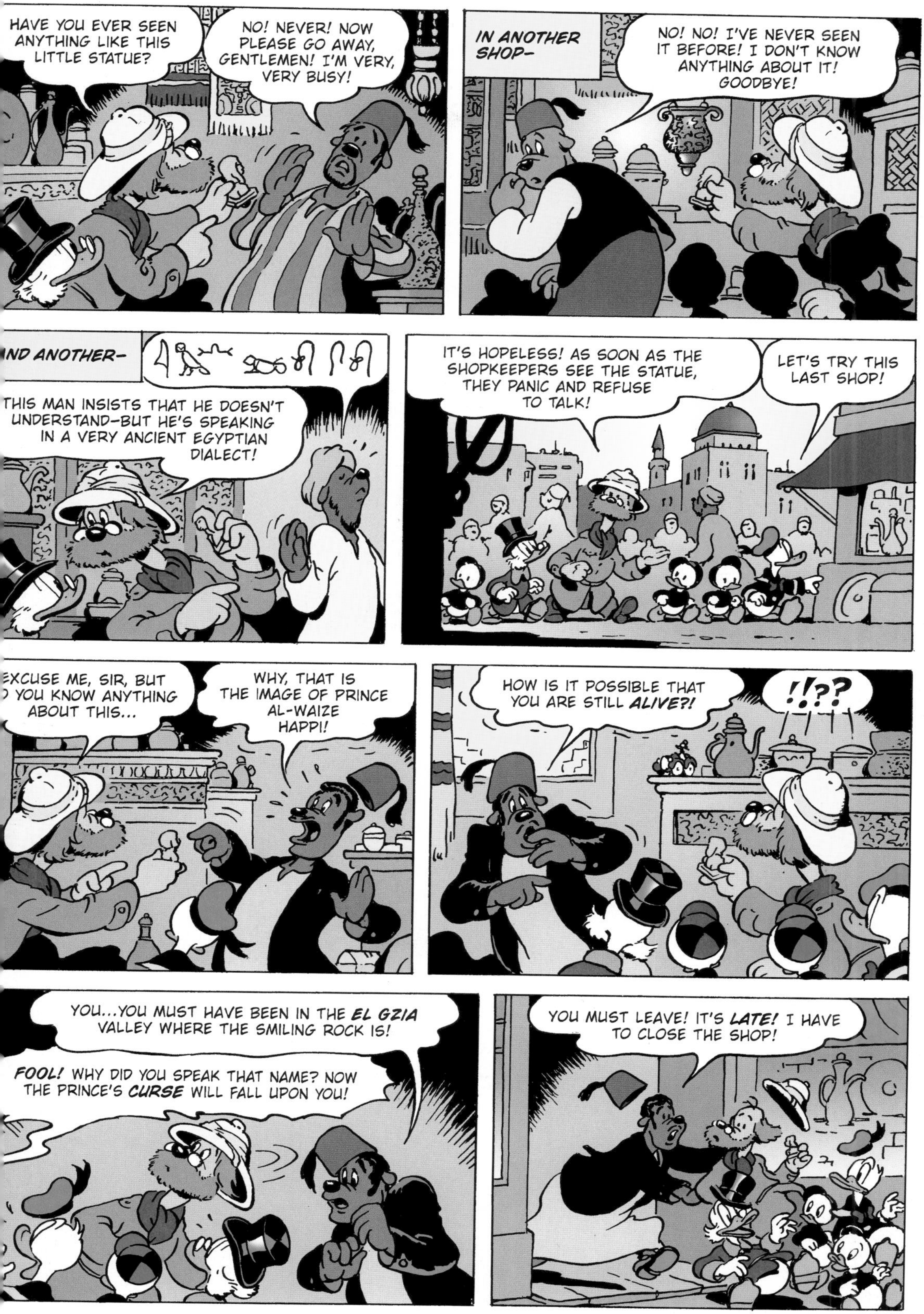
HAVE YOU EVER SEEN ANYTHING LIKE THIS LITTLE STATUE?
NO! NEVER! NOW PLEASE GO AWAY, GENTLEMEN! I'M VERY, VERY BUSY!
IN ANOTHER SHOP–
NO! NO! I'VE NEVER SEEN IT BEFORE! I DON'T KNOW ANYTHING ABOUT IT! GOODBYE!
ND ANOTHER–
THIS MAN INSISTS THAT HE DOESN'T UNDERSTAND–BUT HE'S SPEAKING IN A VERY ANCIENT EGYPTIAN DIALECT!
IT'S HOPELESS! AS SOON AS THE SHOPKEEPERS SEE THE STATUE, THEY PANIC AND REFUSE TO TALK!
LET'S TRY THIS LAST SHOP!
EXCUSE ME, SIR, BUT YOU KNOW ANYTHING ABOUT THIS...
WHY, THAT IS THE IMAGE OF PRINCE AL-WAIZE HAPPI!
HOW IS IT POSSIBLE THAT YOU ARE STILL ALIVE?!
!!??
YOU...YOU MUST HAVE BEEN IN THE EL GZIA VALLEY WHERE THE SMILING ROCK IS!
FOOL! WHY DID YOU SPEAK THAT NAME? NOW THE PRINCE'S CURSE WILL FALL UPON YOU!
YOU MUST LEAVE! IT'S LATE! I HAVE TO CLOSE THE SHOP!

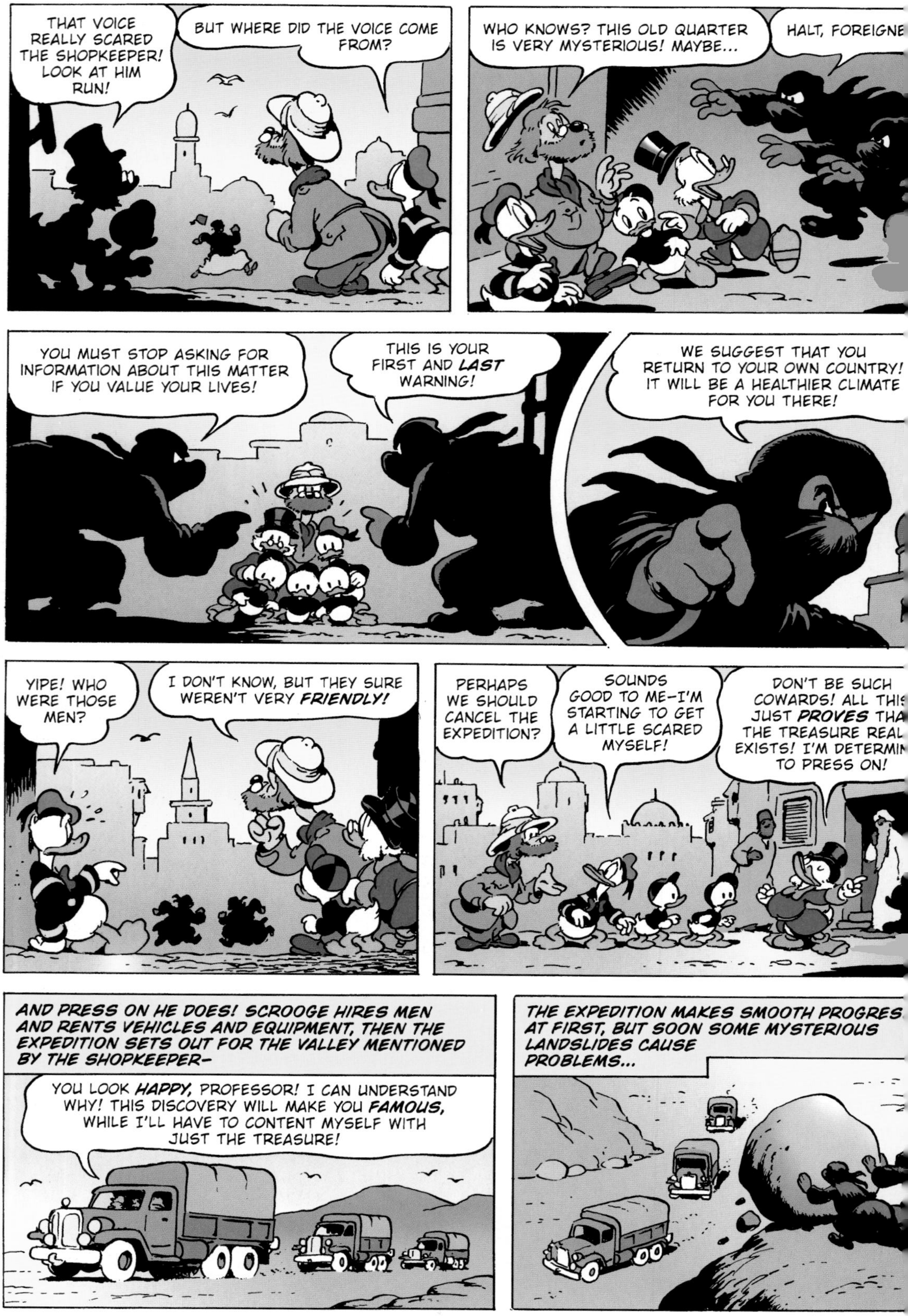
THAT VOICE REALLY SCARED THE SHOPKEEPER! LOOK AT HIM RUN!
BUT WHERE DID THE VOICE COME FROM?
WHO KNOWS? THIS OLD QUARTER IS VERY MYSTERIOUS! MAYBE...
HALT, FOREIGNE
YOU MUST STOP ASKING FOR INFORMATION ABOUT THIS MATTER IF YOU VALUE YOUR LIVES!
THIS IS YOUR FIRST AND LAST WARNING!
WE SUGGEST THAT YOU RETURN TO YOUR OWN COUNTRY! IT WILL BE A HEALTHIER CLIMATE FOR YOU THERE!
YIPE! WHO WERE THOSE MEN?
I DON'T KNOW, BUT THEY SURE WEREN'T VERY FRIENDLY!
PERHAPS WE SHOULD CANCEL THE EXPEDITION?
SOUNDS GOOD TO ME–I'M STARTING TO GET A LITTLE SCARED MYSELF!
DON'T BE SUCH COWARDS! ALL THIS JUST PROVES THA THE TREASURE REAL EXISTS! I'M DETERMIN TO PRESS ON!
AND PRESS ON HE DOES! SCROOGE HIRES MEN AND RENTS VEHICLES AND EQUIPMENT, THEN THE EXPEDITION SETS OUT FOR THE VALLEY MENTIONED BY THE SHOPKEEPER–
YOU LOOK HAPPY, PROFESSOR! I CAN UNDERSTAND WHY! THIS DISCOVERY WILL MAKE YOU FAMOUS, WHILE I'LL HAVE TO CONTENT MYSELF WITH JUST THE TREASURE!
THE EXPEDITION MAKES SMOOTH PROGRES AT FIRST, BUT SOON SOME MYSTERIOUS LANDSLIDES CAUSE PROBLEMS...

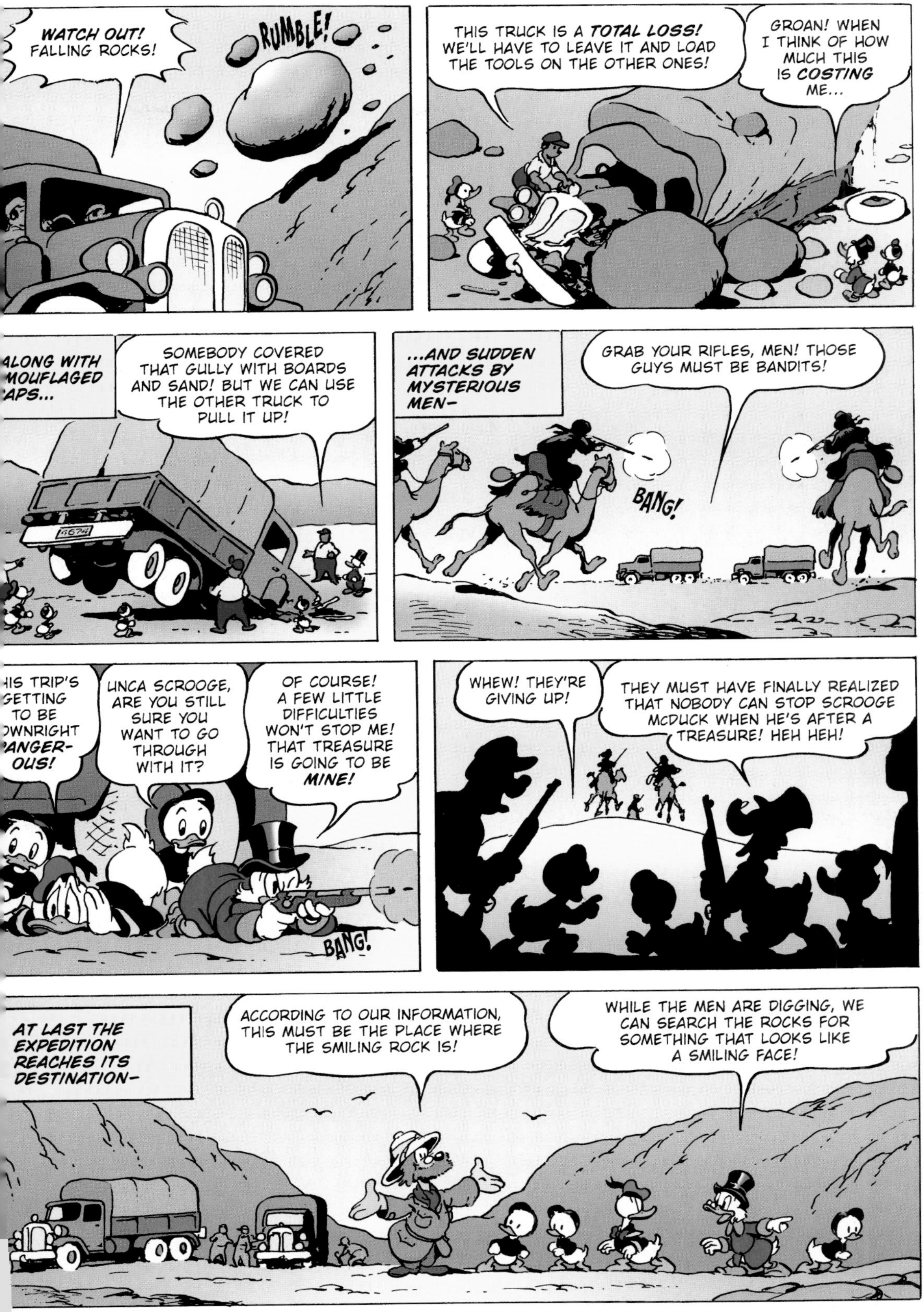
WATCH OUT! FALLING ROCKS!
RUMBLE!
THIS TRUCK IS A TOTAL LOSS! WE'LL HAVE TO LEAVE IT AND LOAD THE TOOLS ON THE OTHER ONES!
GROAN! WHEN I THINK OF HOW MUCH THIS IS COSTING ME...
ALONG WITH MOUFLAGED APS...
SOMEBODY COVERED THAT GULLY WITH BOARDS AND SAND! BUT WE CAN USE THE OTHER TRUCK TO PULL IT UP!
...AND SUDDEN ATTACKS BY MYSTERIOUS MEN–
GRAB YOUR RIFLES, MEN! THOSE GUYS MUST BE BANDITS!
BANG!
HIS TRIP'S GETTING TO BE OWNRIGHT ANGER-OUS!
UNCA SCROOGE, ARE YOU STILL SURE YOU WANT TO GO THROUGH WITH IT?
OF COURSE! A FEW LITTLE DIFFICULTIES WON'T STOP ME! THAT TREASURE IS GOING TO BE MINE!
BANG!
WHEW! THEY'RE GIVING UP!
THEY MUST HAVE FINALLY REALIZED THAT NOBODY CAN STOP SCROOGE McDUCK WHEN HE'S AFTER A TREASURE! HEH HEH!
AT LAST THE EXPEDITION REACHES ITS DESTINATION–
ACCORDING TO OUR INFORMATION, THIS MUST BE THE PLACE WHERE THE SMILING ROCK IS!
WHILE THE MEN ARE DIGGING, WE CAN SEARCH THE ROCKS FOR SOMETHING THAT LOOKS LIKE A SMILING FACE!

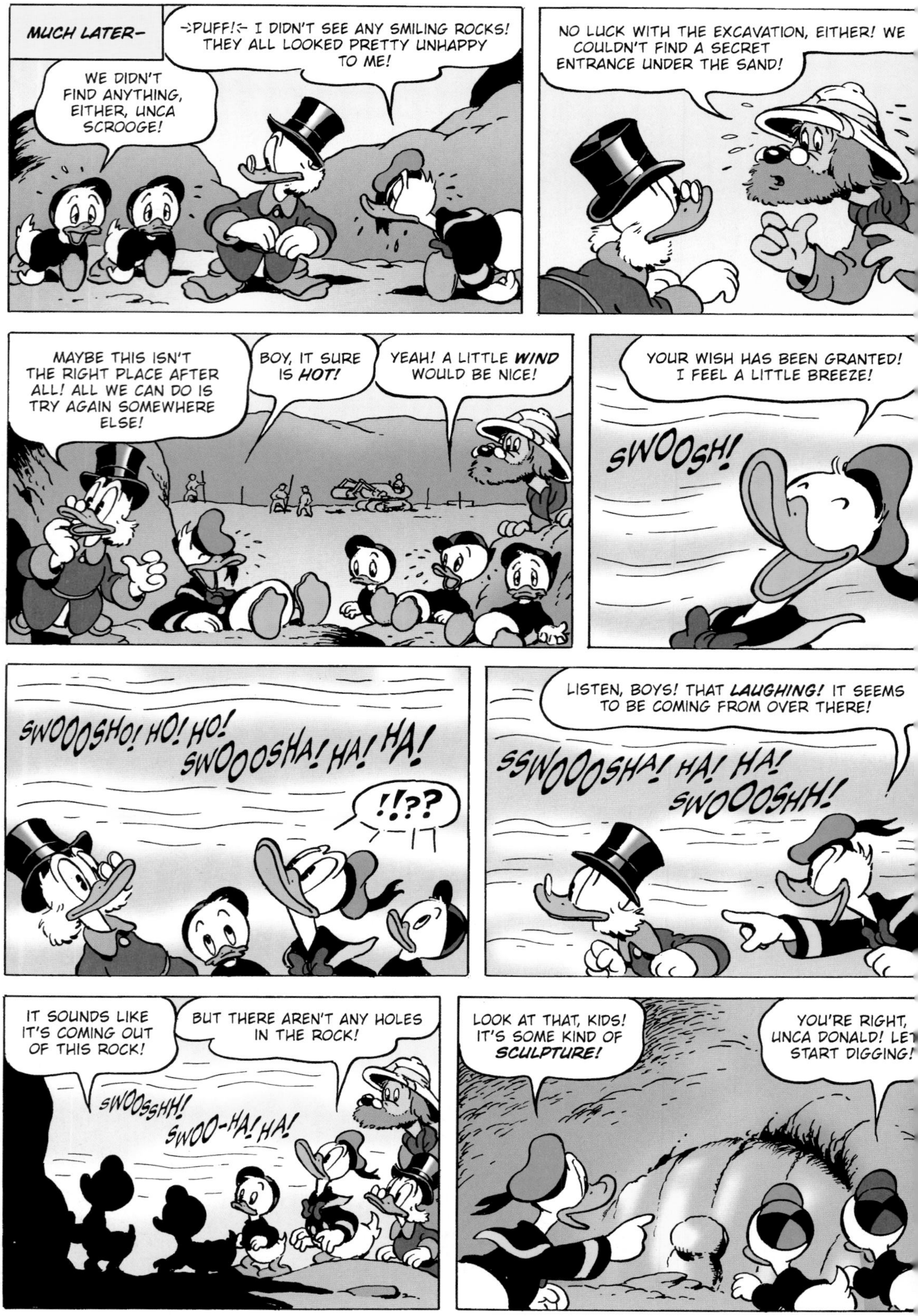
MUCH LATER—
—PUFF!— I DIDN'T SEE ANY SMILING ROCKS! THEY ALL LOOKED PRETTY UNHAPPY TO ME!
WE DIDN'T FIND ANYTHING, EITHER, UNCA SCROOGE!
NO LUCK WITH THE EXCAVATION, EITHER! WE COULDN'T FIND A SECRET ENTRANCE UNDER THE SAND!
MAYBE THIS ISN'T THE RIGHT PLACE AFTER ALL! ALL WE CAN DO IS TRY AGAIN SOMEWHERE ELSE!
BOY, IT SURE IS HOT!
YEAH! A LITTLE WIND WOULD BE NICE!
YOUR WISH HAS BEEN GRANTED! I FEEL A LITTLE BREEZE!
SWOOSH!
SWOOOSHO! HO! HO!
SWOOOSHA! HA! HA!
!!??
LISTEN, BOYS! THAT LAUGHING! IT SEEMS TO BE COMING FROM OVER THERE!
SSWOOOSHA! HA! HA!
SWOOOSHH!
IT SOUNDS LIKE IT'S COMING OUT OF THIS ROCK!
BUT THERE AREN'T ANY HOLES IN THE ROCK!
SWOOSSHH!
SWOO-HA! HA!
LOOK AT THAT, KIDS! IT'S SOME KIND OF SCULPTURE!
YOU'RE RIGHT, UNCA DONALD! LET'S START DIGGING!

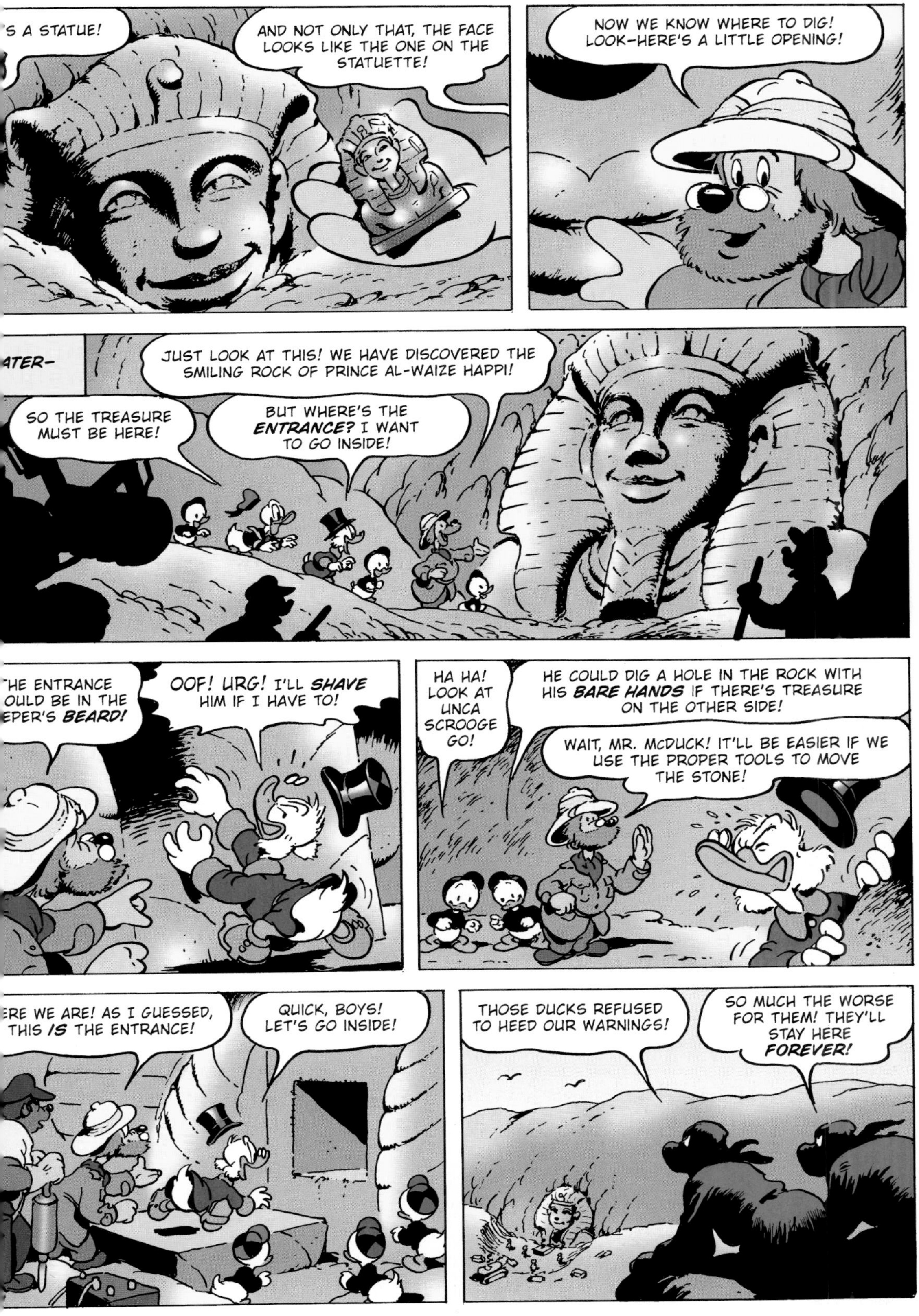

'S A STATUE!
AND NOT ONLY THAT, THE FACE LOOKS LIKE THE ONE ON THE STATUETTE!
NOW WE KNOW WHERE TO DIG! LOOK—HERE'S A LITTLE OPENING!
ATER—
JUST LOOK AT THIS! WE HAVE DISCOVERED THE SMILING ROCK OF PRINCE AL-WAIZE HAPPI!
SO THE TREASURE MUST BE HERE!
BUT WHERE'S THE ENTRANCE? I WANT TO GO INSIDE!
HE ENTRANCE OULD BE IN THE EPER'S BEARD!
OOF! URG! I'LL SHAVE HIM IF I HAVE TO!
HA HA! LOOK AT UNCA SCROOGE GO!
HE COULD DIG A HOLE IN THE ROCK WITH HIS BARE HANDS IF THERE'S TREASURE ON THE OTHER SIDE!
WAIT, MR. McDUCK! IT'LL BE EASIER IF WE USE THE PROPER TOOLS TO MOVE THE STONE!
ERE WE ARE! AS I GUESSED, THIS IS THE ENTRANCE!
QUICK, BOYS! LET'S GO INSIDE!
THOSE DUCKS REFUSED TO HEED OUR WARNINGS!
SO MUCH THE WORSE FOR THEM! THEY'LL STAY HERE FOREVER!

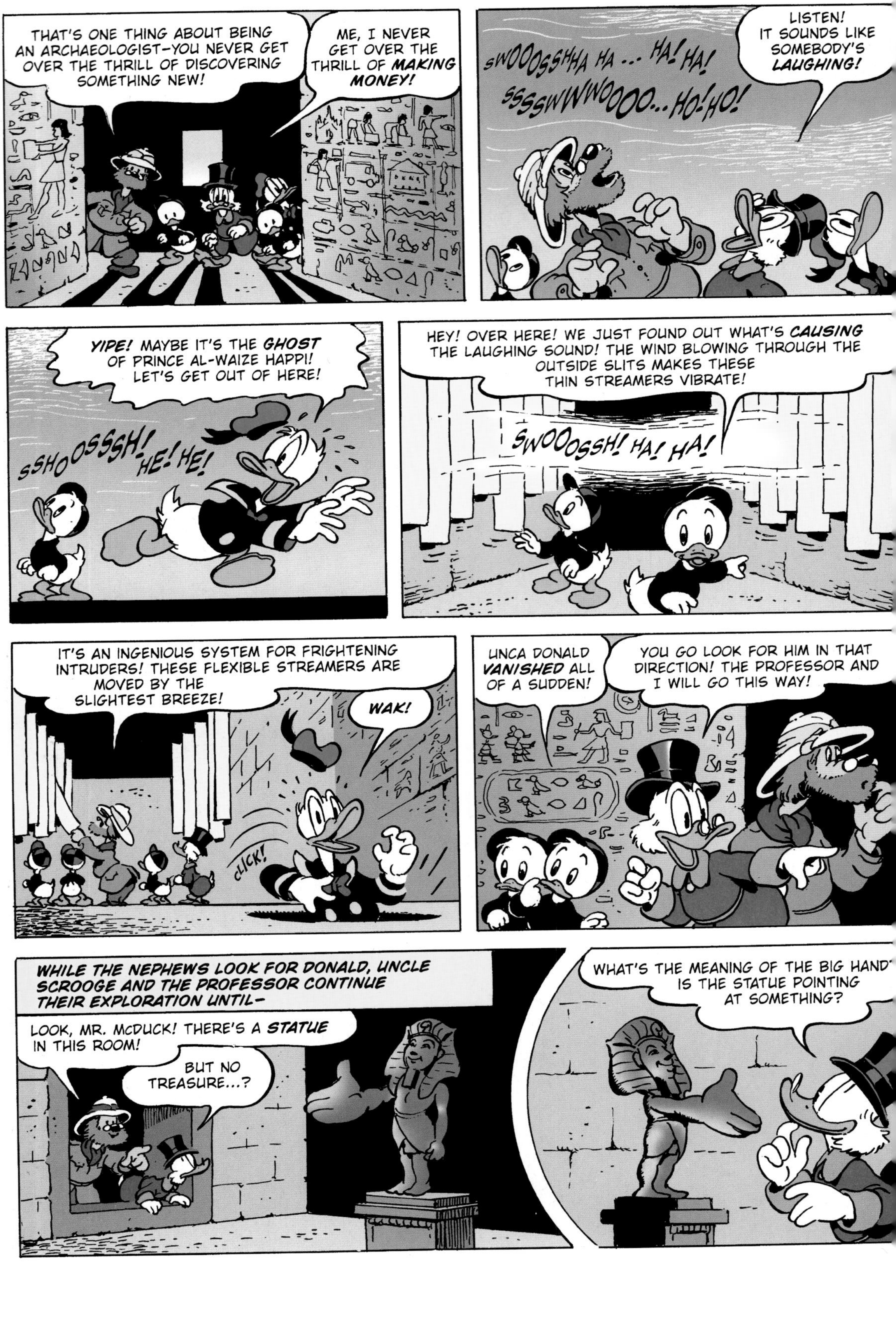

THAT'S ONE THING ABOUT BEING AN ARCHAEOLOGIST–YOU NEVER GET OVER THE THRILL OF DISCOVERING SOMETHING NEW!
ME, I NEVER GET OVER THE THRILL OF MAKING MONEY!
SWOOOSSHHA HA ... HA! HA!
SSSSWWWOOOO...HO! HO!
LISTEN! IT SOUNDS LIKE SOMEBODY'S LAUGHING!
YIPE! MAYBE IT'S THE GHOST OF PRINCE AL-WAIZE HAPPI! LET'S GET OUT OF HERE!
SSHOOSSSH! HE! HE!
HEY! OVER HERE! WE JUST FOUND OUT WHAT'S CAUSING THE LAUGHING SOUND! THE WIND BLOWING THROUGH THE OUTSIDE SLITS MAKES THESE THIN STREAMERS VIBRATE!
SWOOOSSH! HA! HA!
IT'S AN INGENIOUS SYSTEM FOR FRIGHTENING INTRUDERS! THESE FLEXIBLE STREAMERS ARE MOVED BY THE SLIGHTEST BREEZE!
WAK!
CLICK!
UNCA DONALD VANISHED ALL OF A SUDDEN!
YOU GO LOOK FOR HIM IN THAT DIRECTION! THE PROFESSOR AND I WILL GO THIS WAY!
WHILE THE NEPHEWS LOOK FOR DONALD, UNCLE SCROOGE AND THE PROFESSOR CONTINUE THEIR EXPLORATION UNTIL–
LOOK, MR. McDUCK! THERE'S A STATUE IN THIS ROOM!
BUT NO TREASURE...?
WHAT'S THE MEANING OF THE BIG HAND? IS THE STATUE POINTING AT SOMETHING?

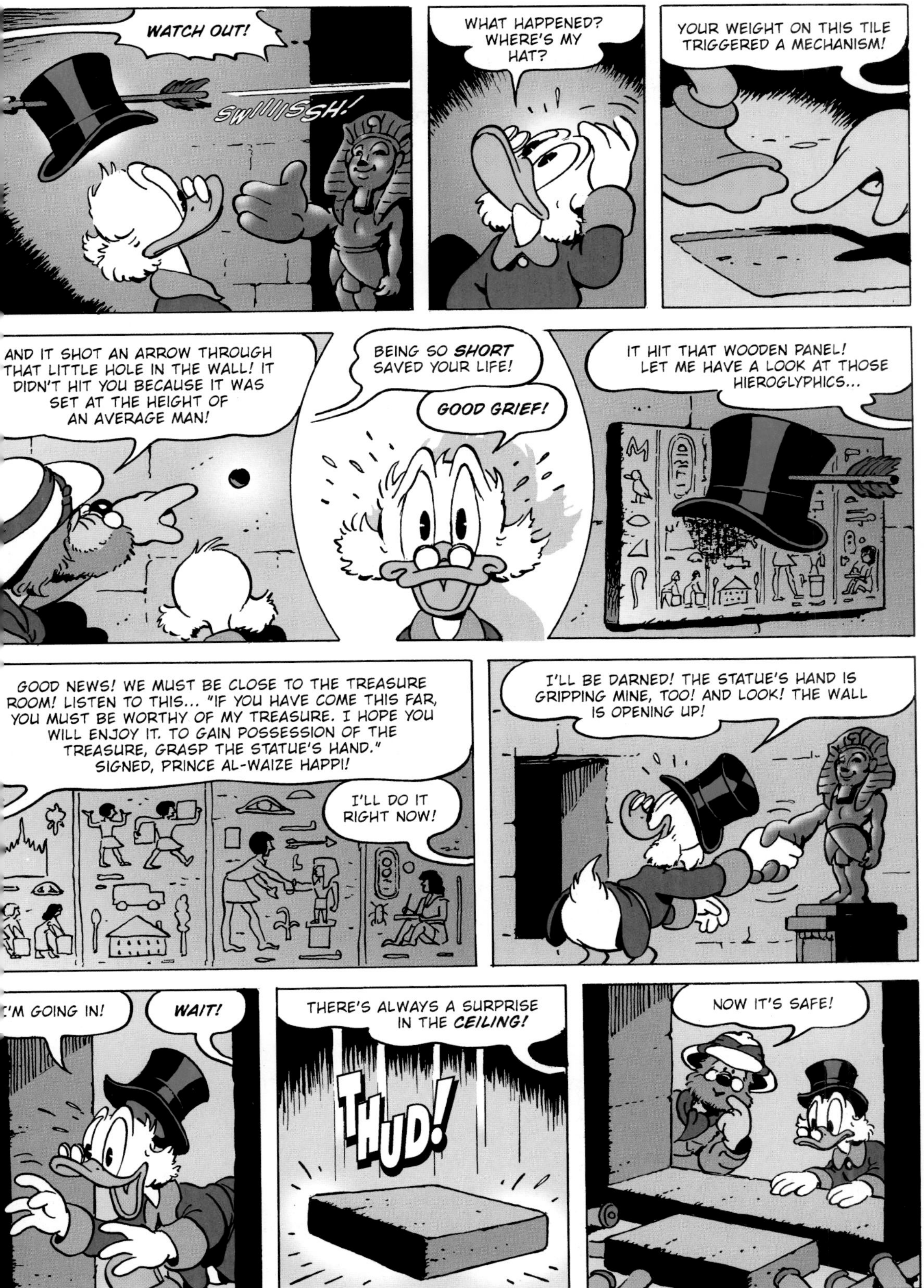
WATCH OUT!
SWIIIISSH!
WHAT HAPPENED? WHERE'S MY HAT?
YOUR WEIGHT ON THIS TILE TRIGGERED A MECHANISM!
AND IT SHOT AN ARROW THROUGH THAT LITTLE HOLE IN THE WALL! IT DIDN'T HIT YOU BECAUSE IT WAS SET AT THE HEIGHT OF AN AVERAGE MAN!
BEING SO SHORT SAVED YOUR LIFE!
GOOD GRIEF!
IT HIT THAT WOODEN PANEL! LET ME HAVE A LOOK AT THOSE HIEROGLYPHICS...
GOOD NEWS! WE MUST BE CLOSE TO THE TREASURE ROOM! LISTEN TO THIS... "IF YOU HAVE COME THIS FAR, YOU MUST BE WORTHY OF MY TREASURE. I HOPE YOU WILL ENJOY IT. TO GAIN POSSESSION OF THE TREASURE, GRASP THE STATUE'S HAND." SIGNED, PRINCE AL-WAIZE HAPPI!
I'LL DO IT RIGHT NOW!
I'LL BE DARNED! THE STATUE'S HAND IS GRIPPING MINE, TOO! AND LOOK! THE WALL IS OPENING UP!
I'M GOING IN!
WAIT!
THERE'S ALWAYS A SURPRISE IN THE CEILING!
THUD!
NOW IT'S SAFE!

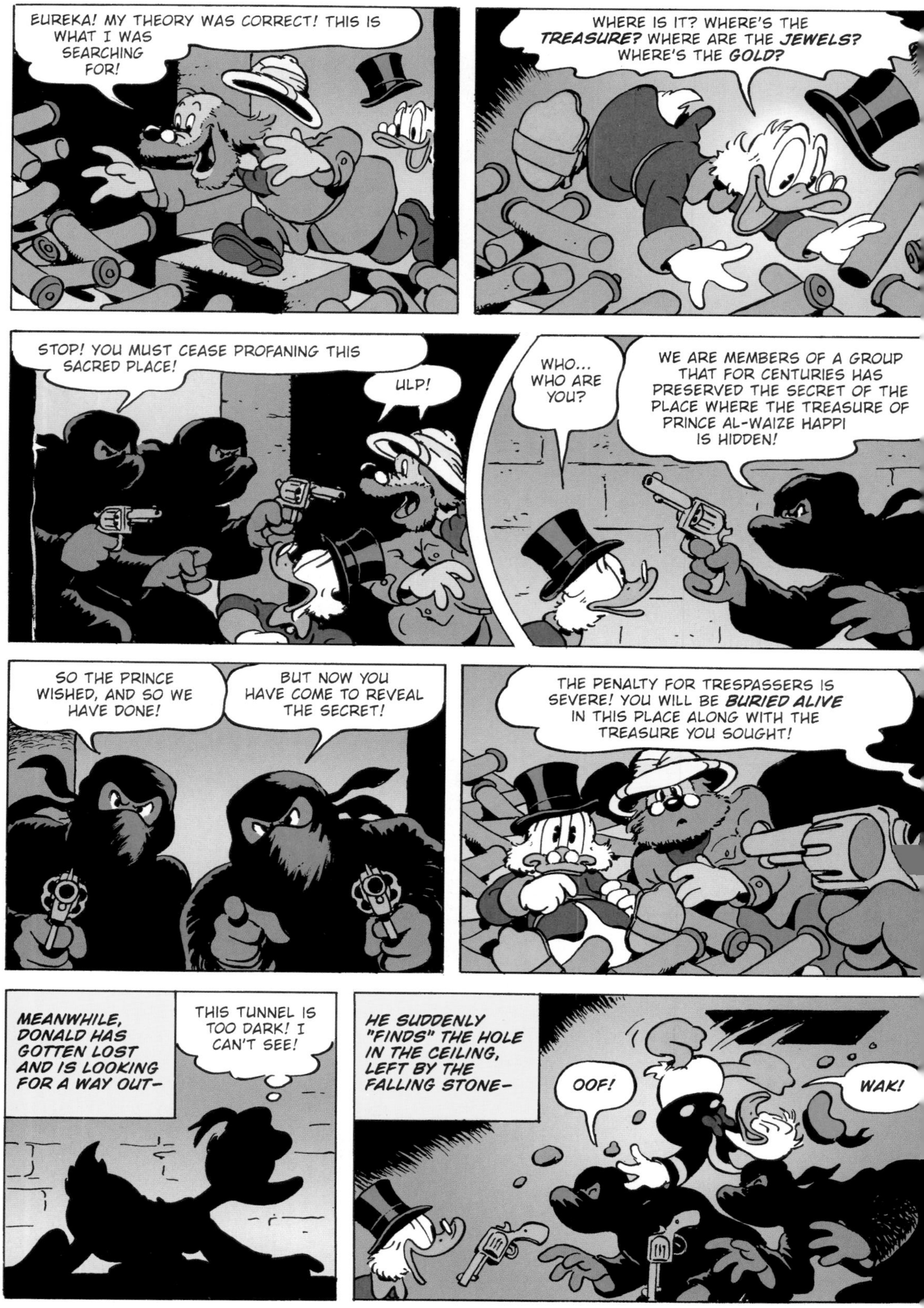
EUREKA! MY THEORY WAS CORRECT! THIS IS WHAT I WAS SEARCHING FOR!
WHERE IS IT? WHERE'S THE TREASURE? WHERE ARE THE JEWELS? WHERE'S THE GOLD?
STOP! YOU MUST CEASE PROFANING THIS SACRED PLACE!
ULP!
WHO... WHO ARE YOU?
WE ARE MEMBERS OF A GROUP THAT FOR CENTURIES HAS PRESERVED THE SECRET OF THE PLACE WHERE THE TREASURE OF PRINCE AL-WAIZE HAPPI IS HIDDEN!
SO THE PRINCE WISHED, AND SO WE HAVE DONE!
BUT NOW YOU HAVE COME TO REVEAL THE SECRET!
THE PENALTY FOR TRESPASSERS IS SEVERE! YOU WILL BE BURIED ALIVE IN THIS PLACE ALONG WITH THE TREASURE YOU SOUGHT!
MEANWHILE, DONALD HAS GOTTEN LOST AND IS LOOKING FOR A WAY OUT–
THIS TUNNEL IS TOO DARK! I CAN'T SEE!
HE SUDDENLY "FINDS" THE HOLE IN THE CEILING, LEFT BY THE FALLING STONE–
OOF!
WAK!

YOU GOT HERE RIGHT ON TIME, NEPHEW! NOW, IF THESE TWO GENTLEMEN WILL JUST PUT THEIR HANDS UP...

DROP THE GUN AND PUT *YOUR* HANDS UP!

OH NO! I DIDN'T SEE THE *THIRD* ONE!

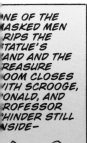

ONE OF THE MASKED MEN GRIPS THE STATUE'S HAND AND THE TREASURE ROOM CLOSES WITH SCROOGE, DONALD, AND PROFESSOR GRINDER STILL INSIDE—

LET'S GO! THE TREASURE IS SAFE ONCE MORE!

NOW WE HAVE TO SEND THE MEN OF THE EXPEDITION AWAY AND HIDE THE ENTRANCE TO THE TOMB AGAIN!

YOU MUST FREE THE PRISONERS OR MY CURSE WILL FALL UPON YOU!

YOU HAVE DONE YOUR WORK WELL, BUT NOW THE TREASURE HAS BEEN DISCOVERED AND YOU NEED PROTECT IT NO LONGER!

THAT'S...THAT'S THE *GHOST* OF PRINCE *AL-WAIZE HAPPI!* WE MUST OBEY!

YOU MUST ALSO HELP THE STRANGERS CARRY THE TREASURE OUT FROM THE HIDING PLACE!

LATER, SCROOGE MAKES ANOTHER ATTEMPT TO SHAKE THE STATUE'S HAND—

ALL THAT'S IN THAT ROOM ARE *PAPYRUS SCROLLS!* THE *REAL* TREASURE ROOM MUST BE SOMEWHERE ELSE! MAYBE THE STATUE WILL SHOW ME WHERE IT IS...

SHAKE!

UH OH! THE STATUE'S HOLDING MY HAND TOO *TIGHT!* URK! I CAN'T GET LOOSE!

SOON—

WHAT KEPT YOU, UNCLE SCROOGE? AND WHY ARE YOU BRINGING THAT THING?

THE STATUE WOULDN'T...ER, LET ME LOOSE, SO I'M TAKING IT WITH ME!

I JUST FOUND AN INTERESTING SCROLL! LISTEN TO THIS!

I HOPE IT TELLS US WHERE THE TREASURE IS!

HA HA! THIS IS GOOD! A MAN SAYS TO ANOTHER MAN: "YOU KNOW, MY IBIS BIRD REALLY SUFFERED WHEN IT LOST A FEATHER!" "WHY?" ASKS THE OTHER MAN...

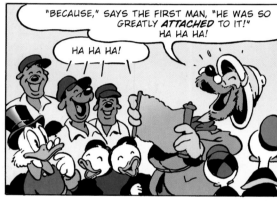

"BECAUSE," SAYS THE FIRST MAN, "HE WAS SO GREATLY *ATTACHED* TO IT!" HA HA HA!

HA HA HA!

AND LISTEN TO THIS ONE! A PAINTER SHOWS A PAINTING TO THE CUSTOMER WHO ORDERED IT, AND SAYS, "HOW DO YOU LIKE THIS PANORAMA OF THE NILE VALLEY?"

AND THE CUSTOMER REPLIES, "BUT THIS PAPYRUS IS ALL *WHITE!* I DON'T SEE ANY PANORAMA!

AND THE PAINTER SAYS, "UNFORTUNATELY, I PAINTED IT ON A *FOGGY DAY!*"

HA HA HA!

!?

HA HA HA!

I DON'T GET IT, PROFESSOR? WHAT *ARE* THESE?

DON'T YOU UNDERSTAND? HA HA! THESE ARE *JOKES!*

JOKES!?

LISTEN! THIS SCROLL EXPLAINS EVERYTHING!

"THE PHARAOH AL-WAIZE ANGRI FORBADE HIS SUBJECTS TO SMILE..."

"...AND SO, EVEN IN THE ROYAL PALACE, ALL THE PEOPLE HAD SAD FACES!"

"MEANWHILE, THE PHARAOH'S BROTHER, PRINCE AL-WAIZE HAPPI, WROTE DOWN MANY JOKES AND SECRETLY READ THEM TO A FEW CLOSE FRIENDS!"

"ONE DAY, THE PHARAOH DISCOVERED THIS AND ORDERED HIM TO DESTROY ALL THE SCROLLS WITH JOKES ON THEM!"

"AS PUNISHMENT, THE PHARAOH SENT THE PRINCE WITH A FEW SOLDIERS TO GUARD THE REMOTE BORDERS IN THE SOUTH OF THE COUNTRY!"

"THE PRINCE TOOK THE SCROLLS WITH HIM BUT DID NOT DESTROY THEM. INSTEAD, HE HAD A TOMB BUILT. IT WAS NOT FOR HIMSELF, HOWEVER, BUT TO HIDE THE SCROLLS AND SO PRESERVE THEM FOREVER!"

LISTEN! IT SOUNDS LIKE THE PRINCE'S WILL!

"I, PRINCE AL-WAIZE HAPPI, GREET THE DISCOVERERS OF MY TREASURE! I HOPE THEY CAN SMILE AS I DID WHEN I WAS ALIVE!"

"THERE WILL BE NO GOLD OR JEWELS IN MY TOMB, FOR I WILL GIVE THEM TO MY SUBJECTS WHILE I STILL LIVE!"

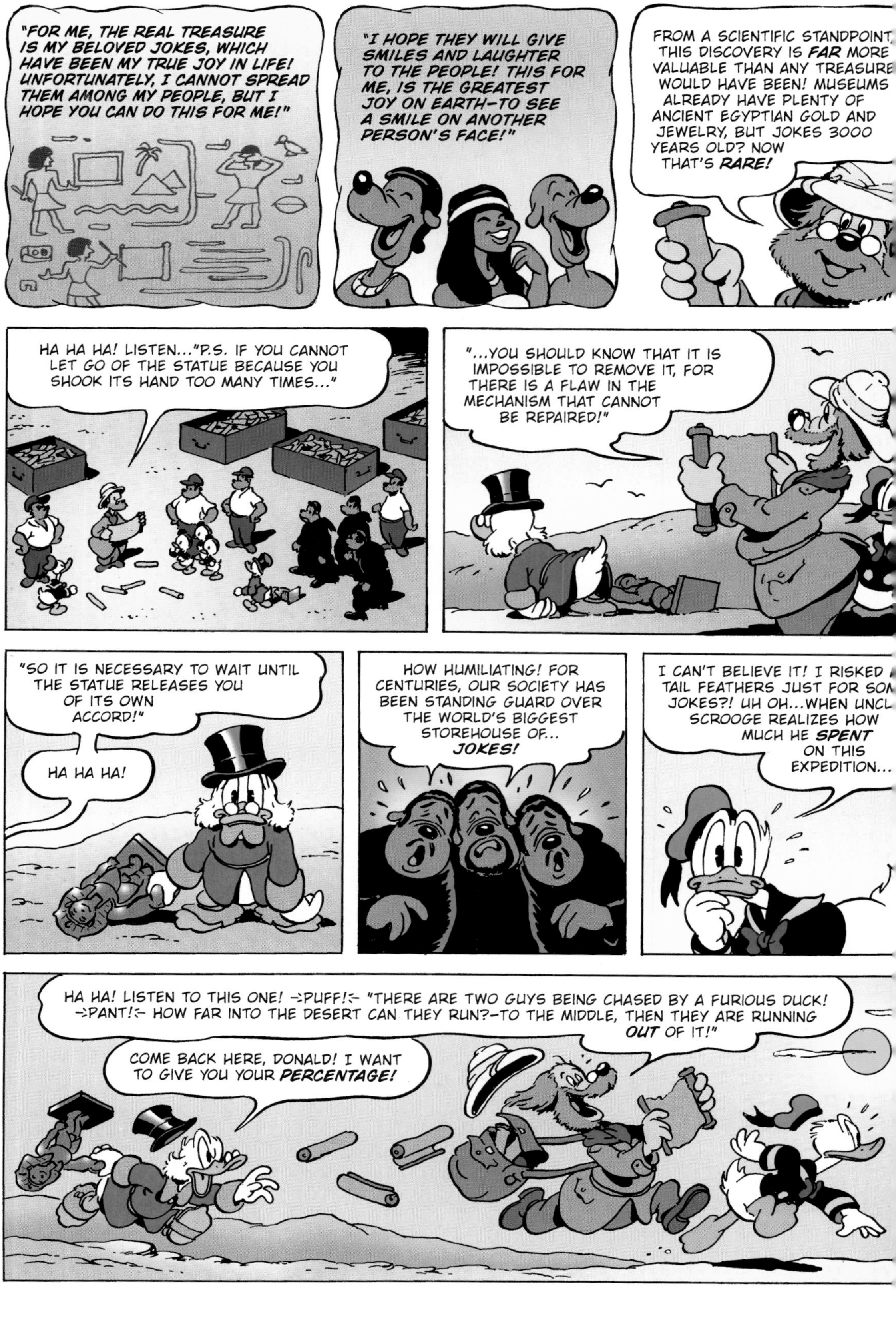
"FOR ME, THE REAL TREASURE IS MY BELOVED JOKES, WHICH HAVE BEEN MY TRUE JOY IN LIFE! UNFORTUNATELY, I CANNOT SPREAD THEM AMONG MY PEOPLE, BUT I HOPE YOU CAN DO THIS FOR ME!"
"I HOPE THEY WILL GIVE SMILES AND LAUGHTER TO THE PEOPLE! THIS FOR ME, IS THE GREATEST JOY ON EARTH—TO SEE A SMILE ON ANOTHER PERSON'S FACE!"
FROM A SCIENTIFIC STANDPOINT, THIS DISCOVERY IS FAR MORE VALUABLE THAN ANY TREASURE WOULD HAVE BEEN! MUSEUMS ALREADY HAVE PLENTY OF ANCIENT EGYPTIAN GOLD AND JEWELRY, BUT JOKES 3000 YEARS OLD? NOW THAT'S RARE!
HA HA HA! LISTEN..."P.S. IF YOU CANNOT LET GO OF THE STATUE BECAUSE YOU SHOOK ITS HAND TOO MANY TIMES..."
"...YOU SHOULD KNOW THAT IT IS IMPOSSIBLE TO REMOVE IT, FOR THERE IS A FLAW IN THE MECHANISM THAT CANNOT BE REPAIRED!"
"SO IT IS NECESSARY TO WAIT UNTIL THE STATUE RELEASES YOU OF ITS OWN ACCORD!"
HA HA HA!
HOW HUMILIATING! FOR CENTURIES, OUR SOCIETY HAS BEEN STANDING GUARD OVER THE WORLD'S BIGGEST STOREHOUSE OF... JOKES!
I CAN'T BELIEVE IT! I RISKED TAIL FEATHERS JUST FOR SO JOKES?! UH OH...WHEN UNCL SCROOGE REALIZES HOW MUCH HE SPENT ON THIS EXPEDITION...
HA HA! LISTEN TO THIS ONE! -PUFF!- "THERE ARE TWO GUYS BEING CHASED BY A FURIOUS DUCK! -PANT!- HOW FAR INTO THE DESERT CAN THEY RUN?—TO THE MIDDLE, THEN THEY ARE RUNNING OUT OF IT!"
COME BACK HERE, DONALD! I WANT TO GIVE YOU YOUR PERCENTAGE!

Walt Disney's

Grandma Duck in She Can Feel It in Her Bones

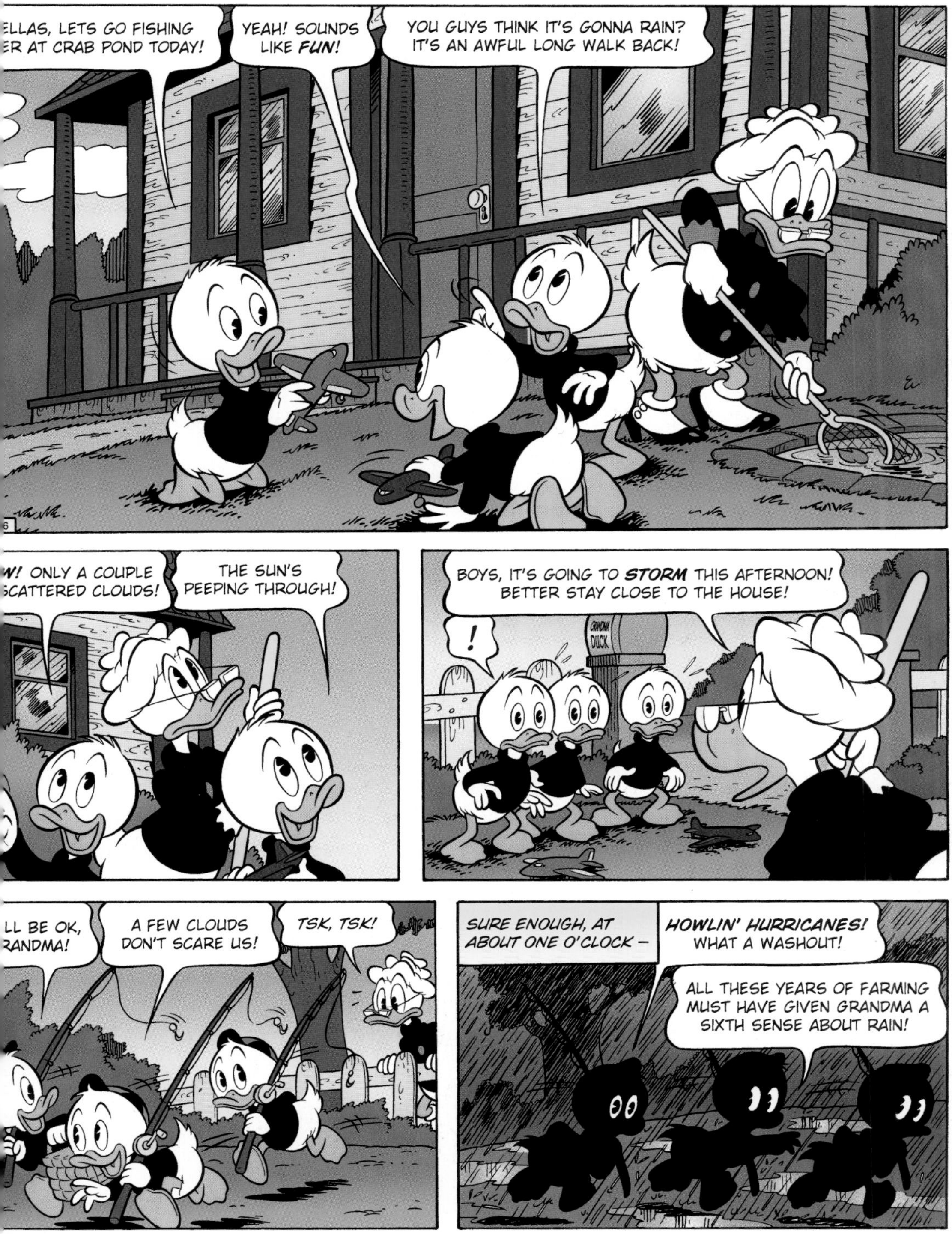

ELLAS, LETS GO FISHING
ER AT CRAB POND TODAY!
YEAH! SOUNDS LIKE FUN!
YOU GUYS THINK IT'S GONNA RAIN? IT'S AN AWFUL LONG WALK BACK!
W! ONLY A COUPLE
SCATTERED CLOUDS!
THE SUN'S PEEPING THROUGH!
BOYS, IT'S GOING TO STORM THIS AFTERNOON! BETTER STAY CLOSE TO THE HOUSE!
!
GRANDMA DUCK
LL BE OK,
RANDMA!
A FEW CLOUDS DON'T SCARE US!
TSK, TSK!
SURE ENOUGH, AT ABOUT ONE O'CLOCK –
HOWLIN' HURRICANES! WHAT A WASHOUT!
ALL THESE YEARS OF FARMING MUST HAVE GIVEN GRANDMA A SIXTH SENSE ABOUT RAIN!

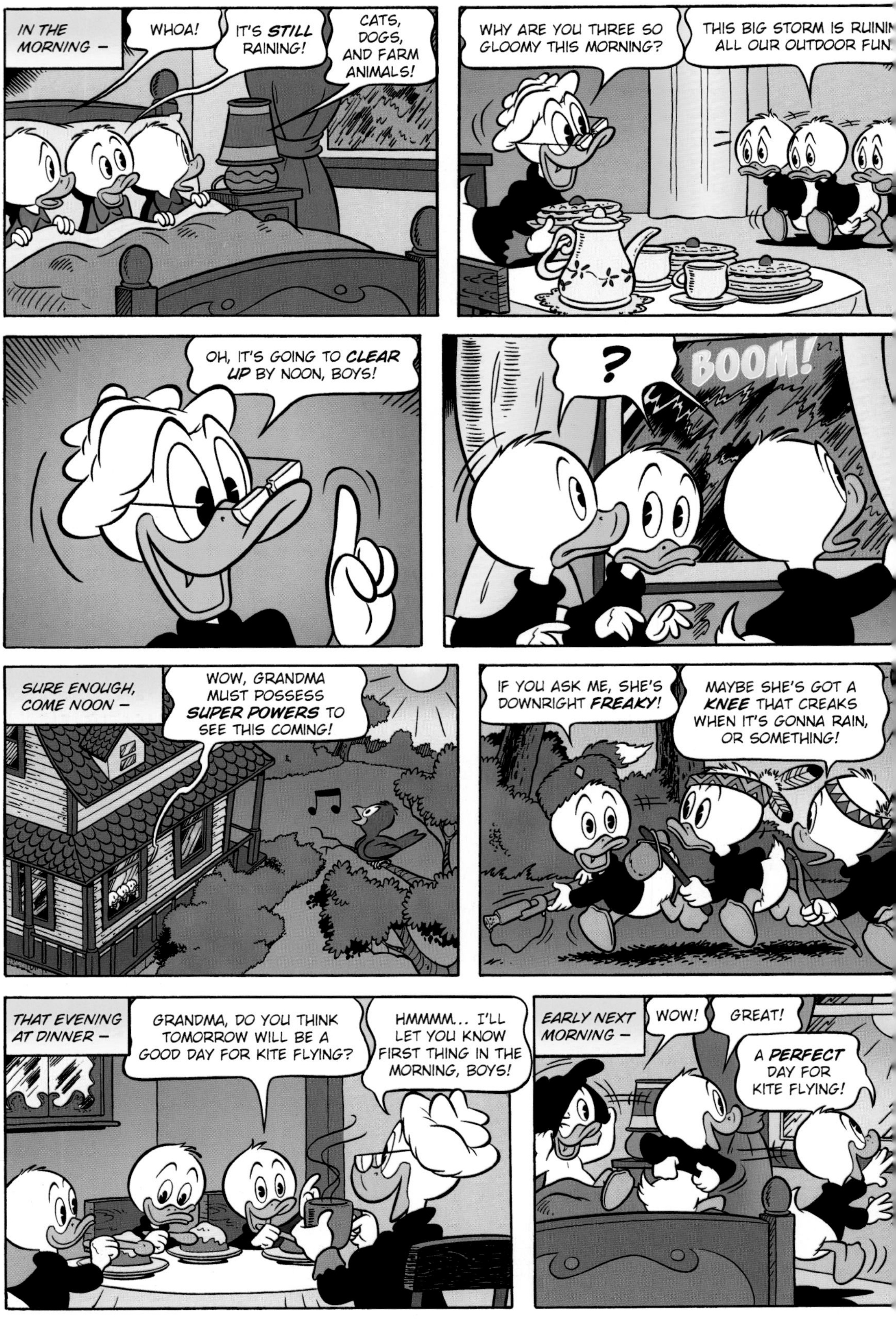
IN THE MORNING —
WHOA!
IT'S STILL RAINING!
CATS, DOGS, AND FARM ANIMALS!
WHY ARE YOU THREE SO GLOOMY THIS MORNING?
THIS BIG STORM IS RUININ ALL OUR OUTDOOR FUN
OH, IT'S GOING TO CLEAR UP BY NOON, BOYS!
?
BOOM!
SURE ENOUGH, COME NOON —
WOW, GRANDMA MUST POSSESS SUPER POWERS TO SEE THIS COMING!
IF YOU ASK ME, SHE'S DOWNRIGHT FREAKY!
MAYBE SHE'S GOT A KNEE THAT CREAKS WHEN IT'S GONNA RAIN, OR SOMETHING!
THAT EVENING AT DINNER —
GRANDMA, DO YOU THINK TOMORROW WILL BE A GOOD DAY FOR KITE FLYING?
HMMMM... I'LL LET YOU KNOW FIRST THING IN THE MORNING, BOYS!
EARLY NEXT MORNING —
WOW!
GREAT!
A PERFECT DAY FOR KITE FLYING!

HMMM... BOYS, I HATE TO SOUND TOO DISCOURAGING, BUT IT'LL BE *WAY TOO WINDY* FOR THAT KITE TODAY!

BUT GRANDMA, IT'S *PERFECT!*

YOU *WANT* WIND FOR KITE FLYING!

WE'RE *BOYS* AND WE *KNOW* GOOD KITE-FLYING WEATHER WHEN WE SEE IT!

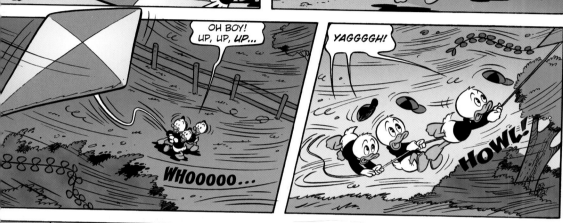

OH BOY! UP, UP, *UP...*

WHOOOOO...

YAGGGGH!

HOWL!

GROAN!

THAT'S THAT!

NO MORE DOUBTS — SHE'S *MOTHER NATURE* HERSELF!

A LIVING *BAROMETER!*

WE'LL BE PLAYING MARBLES UPSTAIRS, GRANDMA!

SOMETHING SAFE THAT DOESN'T INVOLVE BRAVING THE *ELEMENTS!*

AY, BOYS!

OH GOODY! IT'S TIME FOR MY *FAVORITE PROGRAM!*

XYZ TV CHANNEL 9 WEATHER

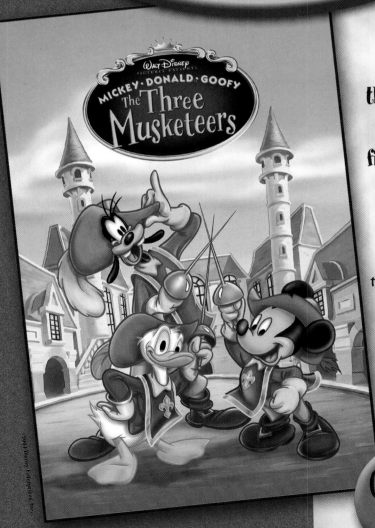

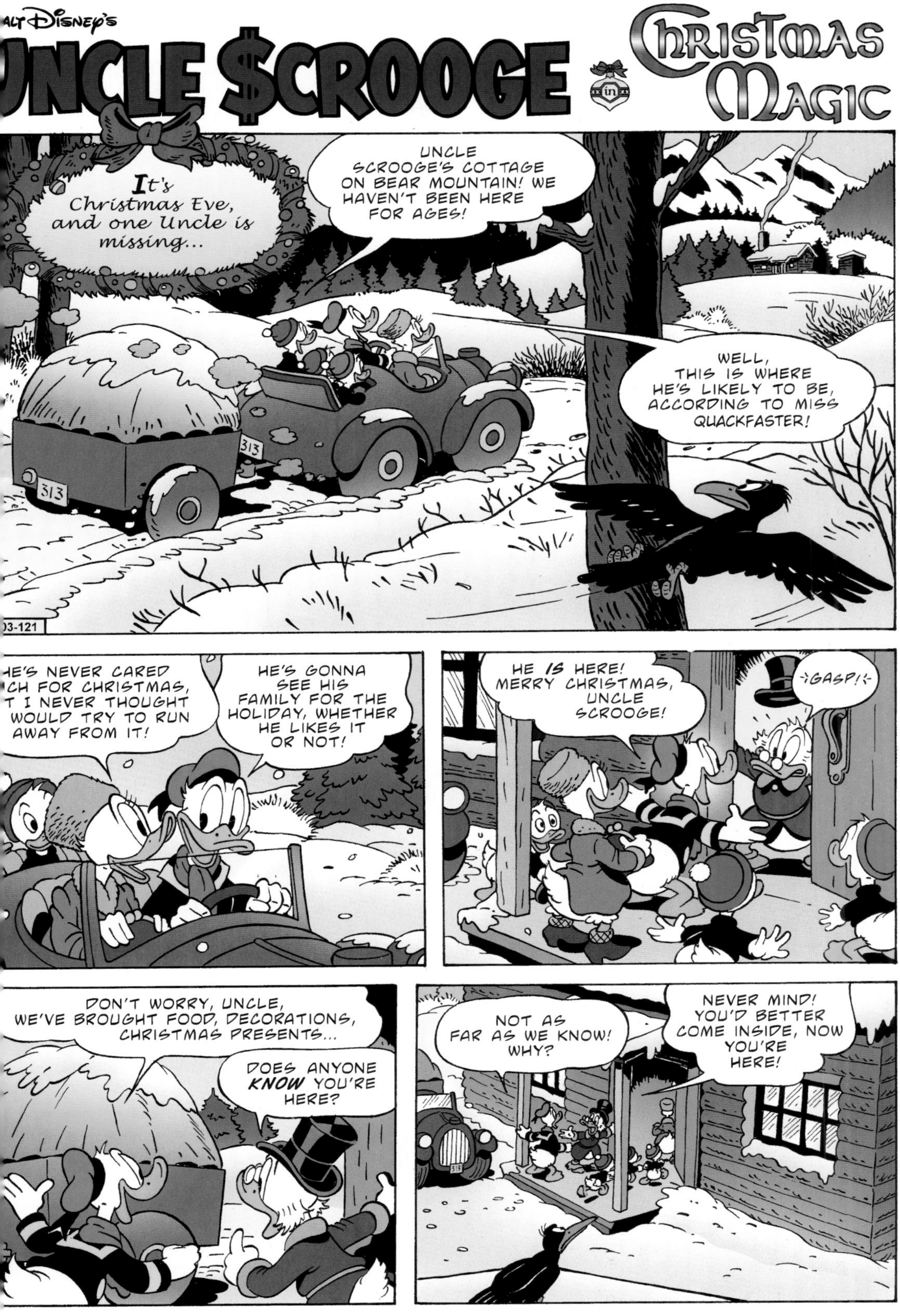
WALT DISNEY'S
UNCLE $CROOGE
in
CHRISTMAS MAGIC
It's Christmas Eve, and one Uncle is missing...
UNCLE SCROOGE'S COTTAGE ON BEAR MOUNTAIN! WE HAVEN'T BEEN HERE FOR AGES!
WELL, THIS IS WHERE HE'S LIKELY TO BE, ACCORDING TO MISS QUACKFASTER!
313
313
D3-121
HE'S NEVER CARED CH FOR CHRISTMAS, T I NEVER THOUGHT WOULD TRY TO RUN AWAY FROM IT!
HE'S GONNA SEE HIS FAMILY FOR THE HOLIDAY, WHETHER HE LIKES IT OR NOT!
HE *IS* HERE! MERRY CHRISTMAS, UNCLE SCROOGE!
GASP!
DON'T WORRY, UNCLE, WE'VE BROUGHT FOOD, DECORATIONS, CHRISTMAS PRESENTS...
DOES ANYONE *KNOW* YOU'RE HERE?
NOT AS FAR AS WE KNOW! WHY?
NEVER MIND! YOU'D BETTER COME INSIDE, NOW YOU'RE HERE!

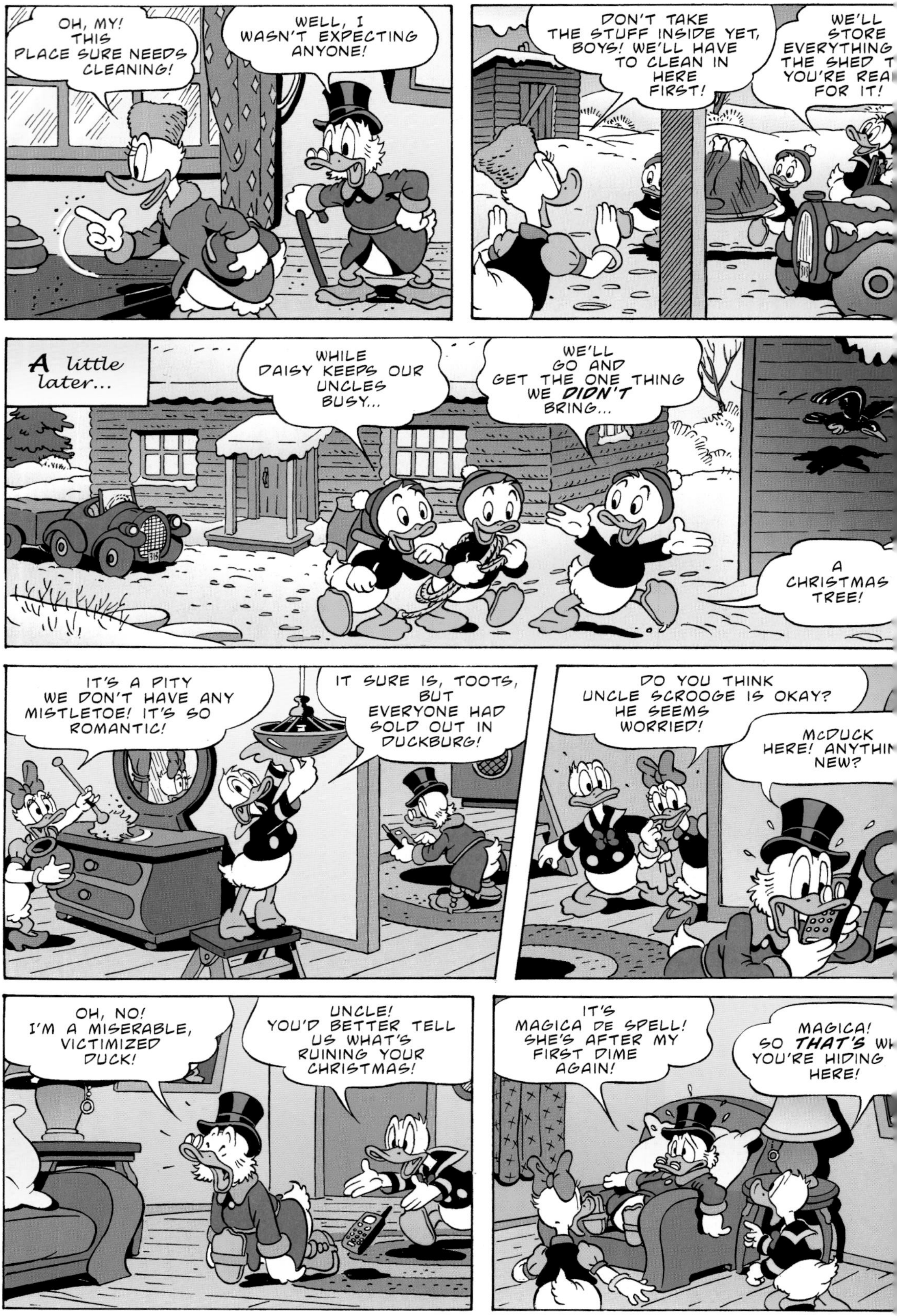

OH, MY! THIS PLACE SURE NEEDS CLEANING!
WELL, I WASN'T EXPECTING ANYONE!
DON'T TAKE THE STUFF INSIDE YET, BOYS! WE'LL HAVE TO CLEAN IN HERE FIRST!
WE'LL STORE EVERYTHING THE SHED T YOU'RE REA FOR IT!
A little later...
WHILE DAISY KEEPS OUR UNCLES BUSY...
WE'LL GO AND GET THE ONE THING WE DIDN'T BRING...
A CHRISTMAS TREE!
IT'S A PITY WE DON'T HAVE ANY MISTLETOE! IT'S SO ROMANTIC!
IT SURE IS, TOOTS, BUT EVERYONE HAD SOLD OUT IN DUCKBURG!
DO YOU THINK UNCLE SCROOGE IS OKAY? HE SEEMS WORRIED!
McDUCK HERE! ANYTHIN NEW?
OH, NO! I'M A MISERABLE, VICTIMIZED DUCK!
UNCLE! YOU'D BETTER TELL US WHAT'S RUINING YOUR CHRISTMAS!
IT'S MAGICA DE SPELL! SHE'S AFTER MY FIRST DIME AGAIN!
MAGICA! SO THAT'S WH YOU'RE HIDING HERE!

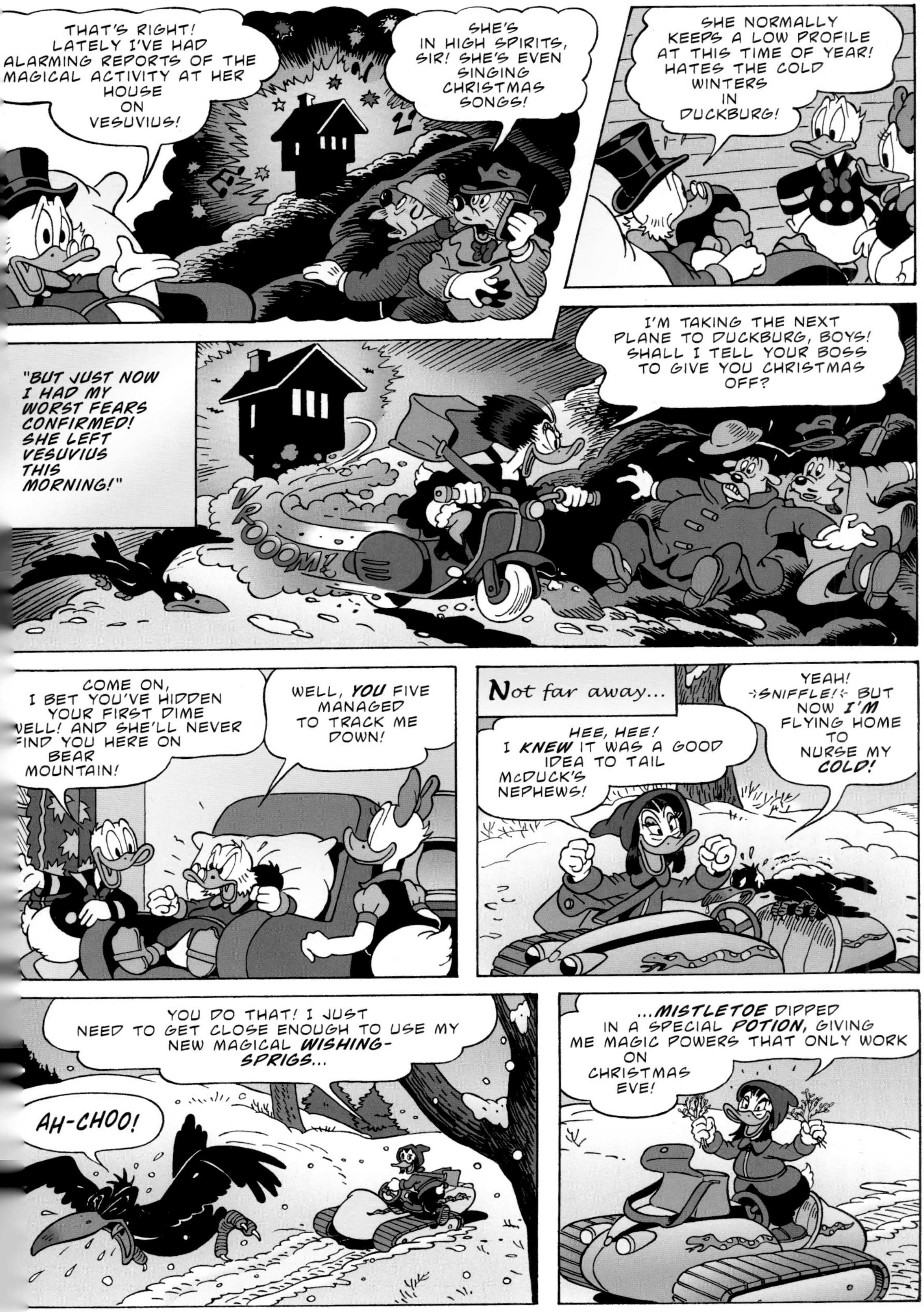
THAT'S RIGHT! LATELY I'VE HAD ALARMING REPORTS OF THE MAGICAL ACTIVITY AT HER HOUSE ON VESUVIUS!
SHE'S IN HIGH SPIRITS, SIR! SHE'S EVEN SINGING CHRISTMAS SONGS!
SHE NORMALLY KEEPS A LOW PROFILE AT THIS TIME OF YEAR! HATES THE COLD WINTERS IN DUCKBURG!
"BUT JUST NOW I HAD MY WORST FEARS CONFIRMED! SHE LEFT VESUVIUS THIS MORNING!"
I'M TAKING THE NEXT PLANE TO DUCKBURG, BOYS! SHALL I TELL YOUR BOSS TO GIVE YOU CHRISTMAS OFF?
VROOOOM!
COME ON, I BET YOU'VE HIDDEN YOUR FIRST DIME WELL! AND SHE'LL NEVER FIND YOU HERE ON BEAR MOUNTAIN!
WELL, YOU FIVE MANAGED TO TRACK ME DOWN!
Not far away...
HEE, HEE! I KNEW IT WAS A GOOD IDEA TO TAIL McDUCK'S NEPHEWS!
YEAH! SNIFFLE! BUT NOW I'M FLYING HOME TO NURSE MY COLD!
YOU DO THAT! I JUST NEED TO GET CLOSE ENOUGH TO USE MY NEW MAGICAL WISHING-SPRIGS...
AH-CHOO!
...MISTLETOE DIPPED IN A SPECIAL POTION, GIVING ME MAGIC POWERS THAT ONLY WORK ON CHRISTMAS EVE!

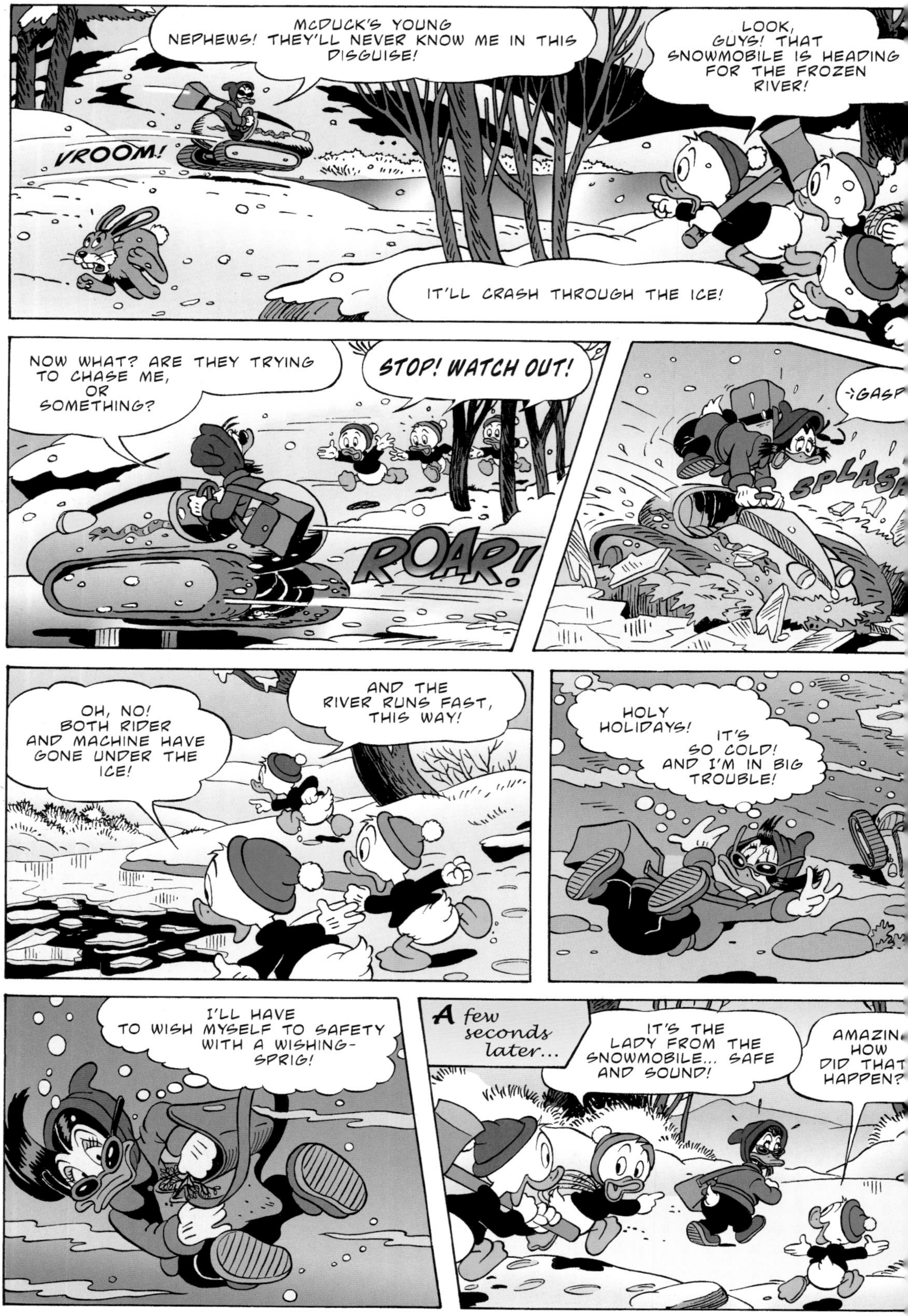
McDUCK'S YOUNG NEPHEWS! THEY'LL NEVER KNOW ME IN THIS DISGUISE!
VROOM!
LOOK, GUYS! THAT SNOWMOBILE IS HEADING FOR THE FROZEN RIVER!
IT'LL CRASH THROUGH THE ICE!
NOW WHAT? ARE THEY TRYING TO CHASE ME, OR SOMETHING?
STOP! WATCH OUT!
ROAR!
GASP
SPLASH
OH, NO! BOTH RIDER AND MACHINE HAVE GONE UNDER THE ICE!
AND THE RIVER RUNS FAST, THIS WAY!
HOLY HOLIDAYS! IT'S SO COLD! AND I'M IN BIG TROUBLE!
I'LL HAVE TO WISH MYSELF TO SAFETY WITH A WISHING-SPRIG!
A few seconds later...
IT'S THE LADY FROM THE SNOWMOBILE... SAFE AND SOUND!
AMAZIN HOW DID THAT HAPPEN?

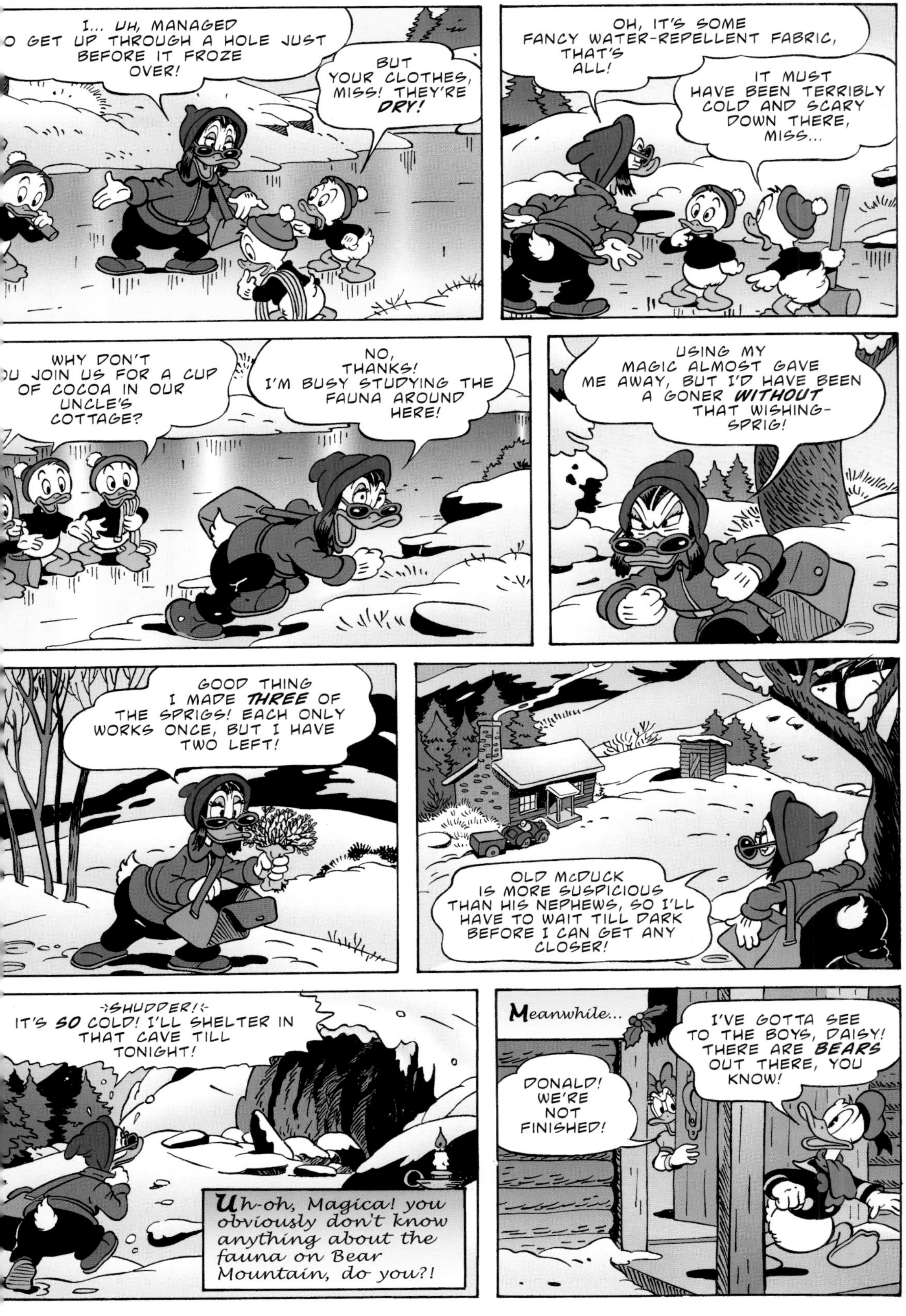
I... UH, MANAGED O GET UP THROUGH A HOLE JUST BEFORE IT FROZE OVER!
BUT YOUR CLOTHES, MISS! THEY'RE *DRY!*
OH, IT'S SOME FANCY WATER-REPELLENT FABRIC, THAT'S ALL!
IT MUST HAVE BEEN TERRIBLY COLD AND SCARY DOWN THERE, MISS...
WHY DON'T OU JOIN US FOR A CUP OF COCOA IN OUR UNCLE'S COTTAGE?
NO, THANKS! I'M BUSY STUDYING THE FAUNA AROUND HERE!
USING MY MAGIC ALMOST GAVE ME AWAY, BUT I'D HAVE BEEN A GONER ***WITHOUT*** THAT WISHING-SPRIG!
GOOD THING I MADE ***THREE*** OF THE SPRIGS! EACH ONLY WORKS ONCE, BUT I HAVE TWO LEFT!
OLD McDUCK IS MORE SUSPICIOUS THAN HIS NEPHEWS, SO I'LL HAVE TO WAIT TILL DARK BEFORE I CAN GET ANY CLOSER!
-SHUDDER!- IT'S ***SO*** COLD! I'LL SHELTER IN THAT CAVE TILL TONIGHT!
Uh-oh, Magica! you obviously don't know anything about the fauna on Bear Mountain, do you?!
Meanwhile...
I'VE GOTTA SEE TO THE BOYS, DAISY! THERE ARE ***BEARS*** OUT THERE, YOU KNOW!
DONALD! WE'RE NOT FINISHED!

The boys are fine! And they've found a great Christmas tree!

BUT IT'S TOO TALL FOR UNCA SCROOGE'S COTTAGE!

WE'LL JUST TAKE THE TOP HALF, THEN!

ISN'T IT KINDA STRANGE TO STUDY FAUNA ON CHRISTMAS EVE? WHAT KIND OF ANIMALS COULD THAT LADY BE AFTER?

NOT *BEARS*, THAT'S FOR SURE...

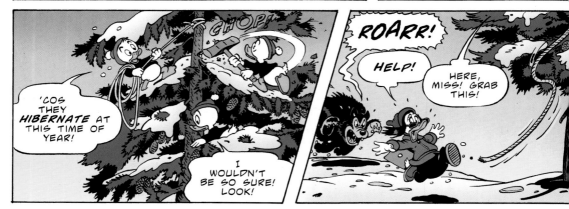

GHOP!

'COS THEY *HIBERNATE* AT THIS TIME OF YEAR!

I WOULDN'T BE SO SURE! LOOK!

ROARR!

HELP!

HERE, MISS! GRAB THIS!

¡GASP!

GROWL?!

URWTY.

OH, HANG IT!

UH-OH! WATCH OUT GUYS!

DARN! SPRIG NUMBER TWO *LOST* OVER THE CLIFF! GOTTA BE *CAREFUL* WITH THE LAST ONE!

¡UHF!

CHOFF!

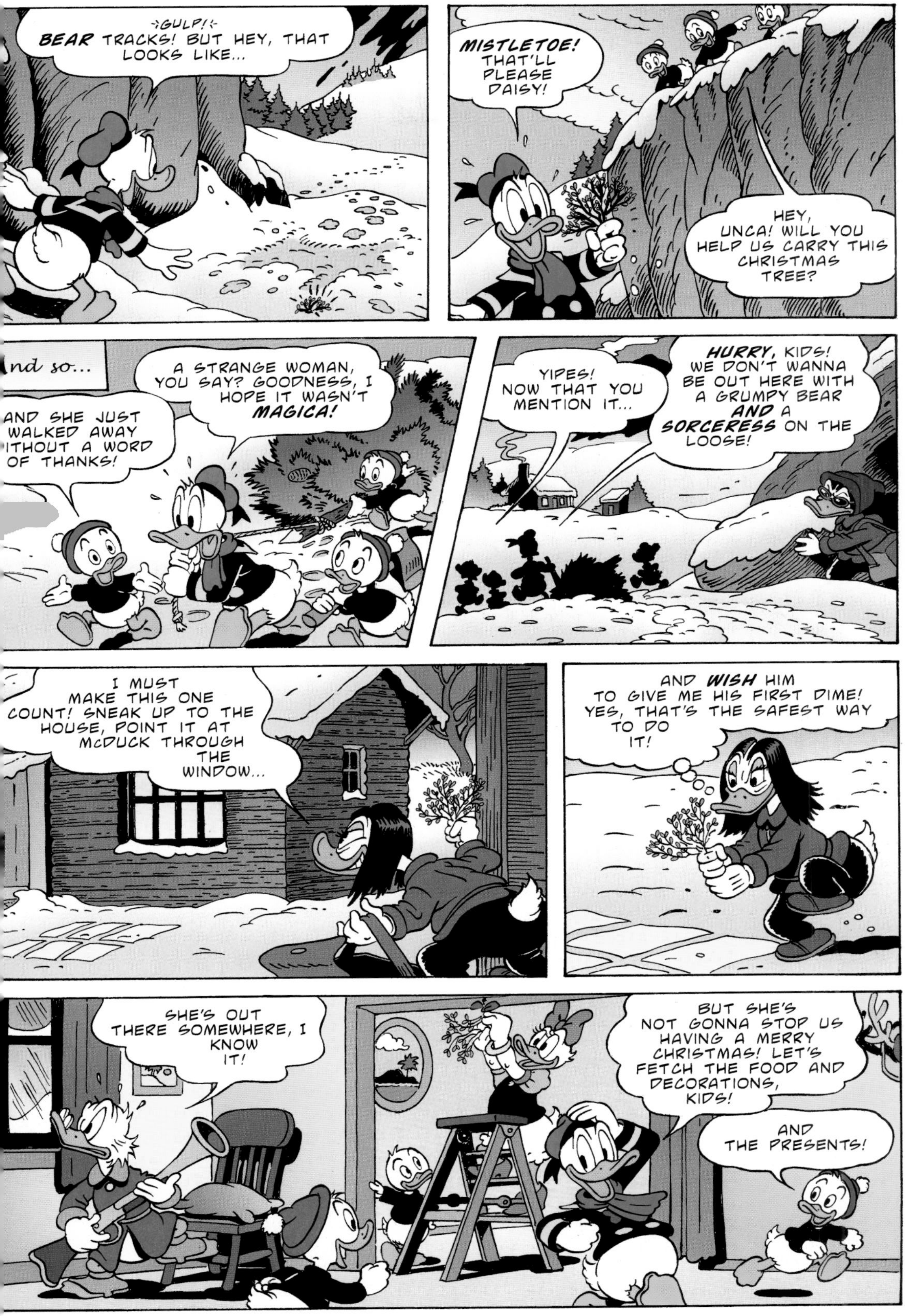

-GULP!-
BEAR TRACKS! BUT HEY, THAT LOOKS LIKE...
MISTLETOE! THAT'LL PLEASE DAISY!
HEY, UNCA! WILL YOU HELP US CARRY THIS CHRISTMAS TREE?
And so...
AND SHE JUST WALKED AWAY ITHOUT A WORD OF THANKS!
A STRANGE WOMAN, YOU SAY? GOODNESS, I HOPE IT WASN'T MAGICA!
YIPES! NOW THAT YOU MENTION IT...
HURRY, KIDS! WE DON'T WANNA BE OUT HERE WITH A GRUMPY BEAR AND A SORCERESS ON THE LOOSE!
I MUST MAKE THIS ONE COUNT! SNEAK UP TO THE HOUSE, POINT IT AT McDUCK THROUGH THE WINDOW...
AND WISH HIM TO GIVE ME HIS FIRST DIME! YES, THAT'S THE SAFEST WAY TO DO IT!
SHE'S OUT THERE SOMEWHERE, I KNOW IT!
BUT SHE'S NOT GONNA STOP US HAVING A MERRY CHRISTMAS! LET'S FETCH THE FOOD AND DECORATIONS, KIDS!
AND THE PRESENTS!

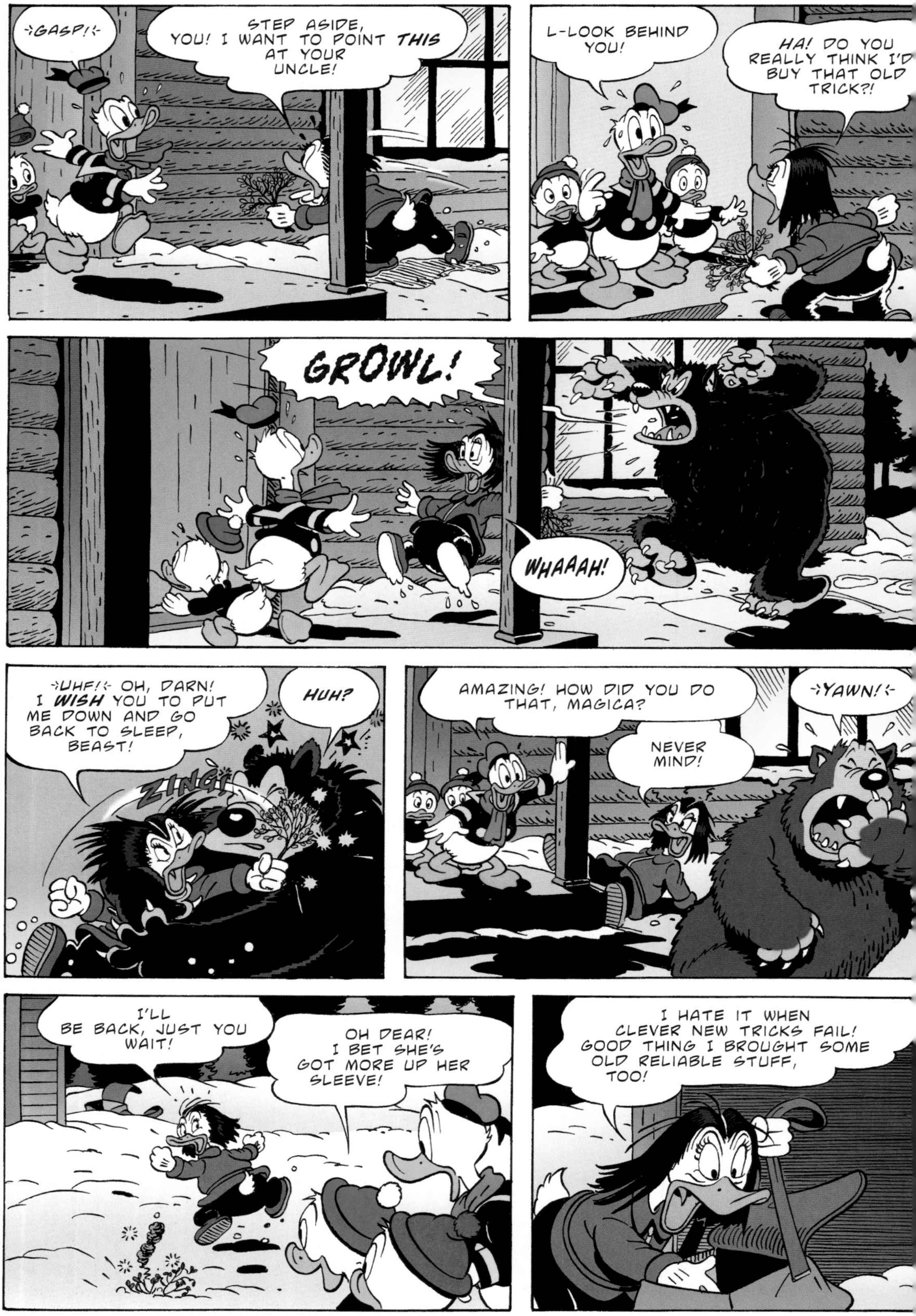

-¦GASP!¦-
STEP ASIDE, YOU! I WANT TO POINT THIS AT YOUR UNCLE!
L-LOOK BEHIND YOU!
HA! DO YOU REALLY THINK I'D BUY THAT OLD TRICK?!
GROWL!
WHAAAH!
-¦UHF!¦- OH, DARN! I WISH YOU TO PUT ME DOWN AND GO BACK TO SLEEP, BEAST!
HUH?
ZING!
AMAZING! HOW DID YOU DO THAT, MAGICA?
NEVER MIND!
-¦YAWN!¦-
I'LL BE BACK, JUST YOU WAIT!
OH DEAR! I BET SHE'S GOT MORE UP HER SLEEVE!
I HATE IT WHEN CLEVER NEW TRICKS FAIL! GOOD THING I BROUGHT SOME OLD RELIABLE STUFF, TOO!

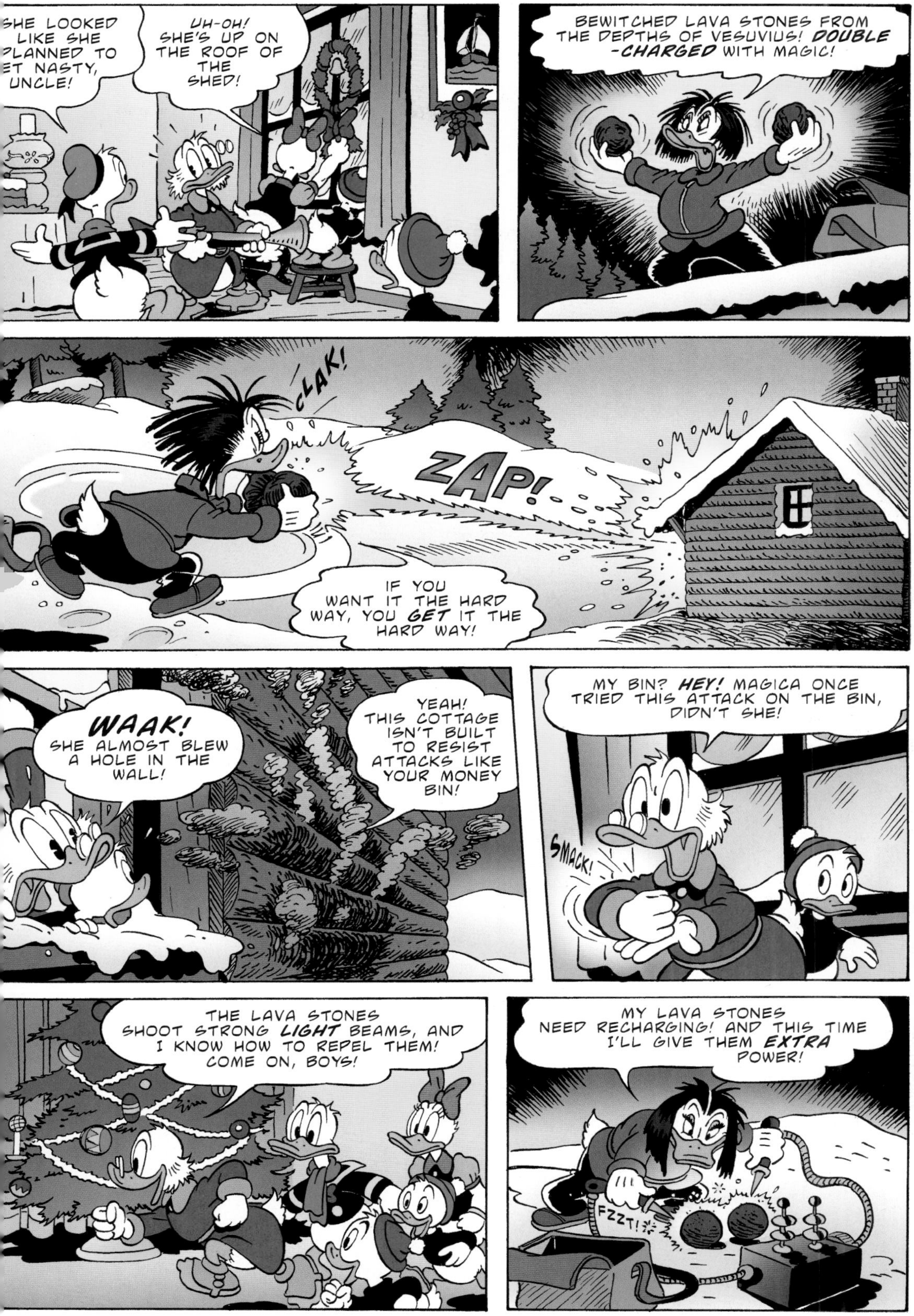

SHE LOOKED LIKE SHE PLANNED TO ET NASTY, UNCLE!
UH-OH! SHE'S UP ON THE ROOF OF THE SHED!
BEWITCHED LAVA STONES FROM THE DEPTHS OF VESUVIUS! DOUBLE-CHARGED WITH MAGIC!
CLAK!
ZAP!
IF YOU WANT IT THE HARD WAY, YOU GET IT THE HARD WAY!
WAAK! SHE ALMOST BLEW A HOLE IN THE WALL!
YEAH! THIS COTTAGE ISN'T BUILT TO RESIST ATTACKS LIKE YOUR MONEY BIN!
MY BIN? HEY! MAGICA ONCE TRIED THIS ATTACK ON THE BIN, DIDN'T SHE!
SMACK!
THE LAVA STONES SHOOT STRONG LIGHT BEAMS, AND I KNOW HOW TO REPEL THEM! COME ON, BOYS!
MY LAVA STONES NEED RECHARGING! AND THIS TIME I'LL GIVE THEM EXTRA POWER!
FZZT!

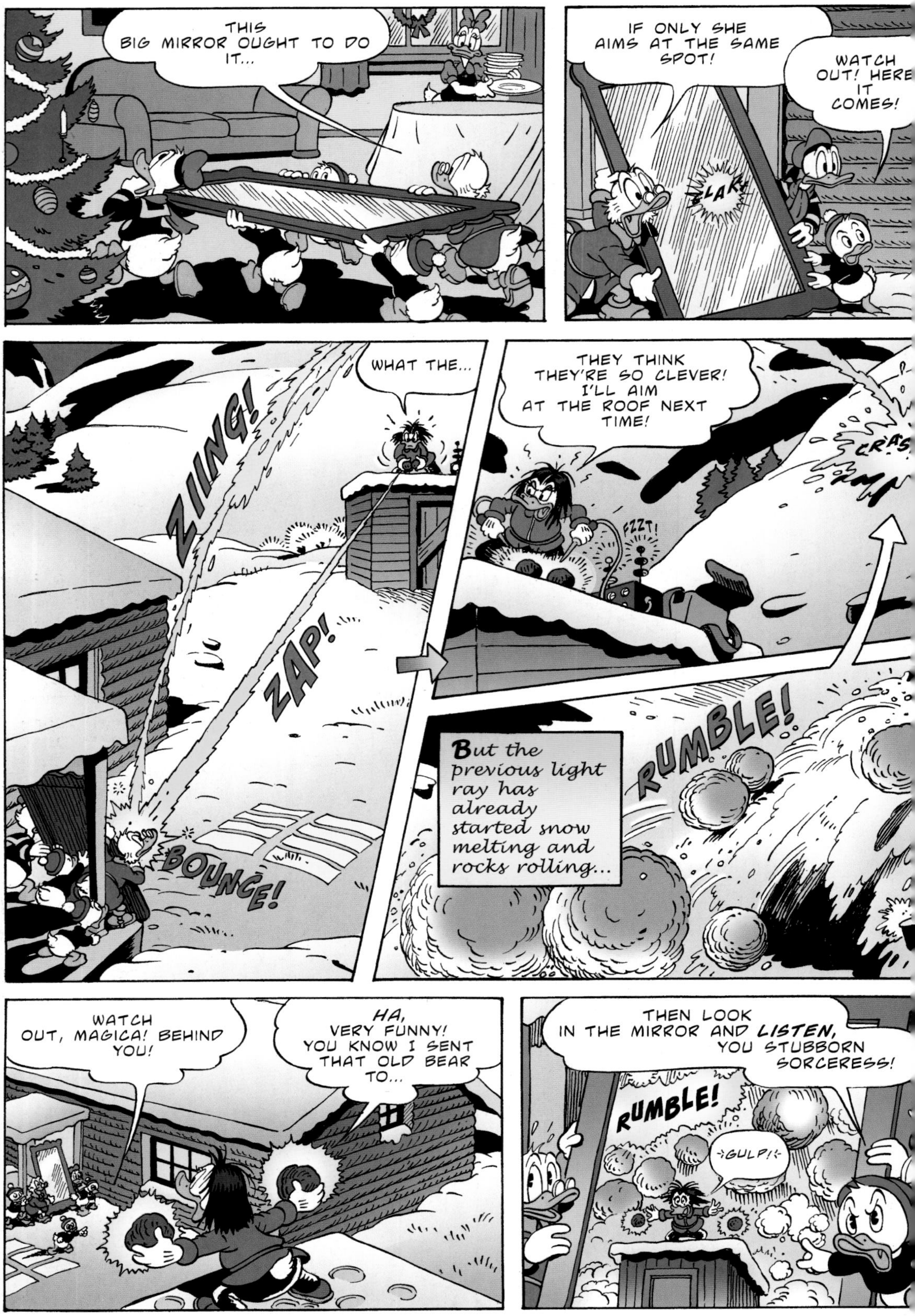

THIS BIG MIRROR OUGHT TO DO IT...
IF ONLY SHE AIMS AT THE SAME SPOT!
WATCH OUT! HERE IT COMES!
BLAK!
WHAT THE...
ZIING!
ZAP!
BOUNCE!
THEY THINK THEY'RE SO CLEVER! I'LL AIM AT THE ROOF NEXT TIME!
FZZT!
But the previous light ray has already started snow melting and rocks rolling...
RUMBLE!
WATCH OUT, MAGICA! BEHIND YOU!
HA, VERY FUNNY! YOU KNOW I SENT THAT OLD BEAR TO...
THEN LOOK IN THE MIRROR AND LISTEN, YOU STUBBORN SORCERESS!
RUMBLE!
GULP!

AARRGH!

GRUNCH!

SHE'S DEFENSELESS! TIE HER UP, BOYS!

MY VOLCANO STONES! ALL MY EQUIPMENT! BURIED UNDER TONS OF ROCK!

YOU KNOW WHAT? OUR *CHRISTMAS* HAS BEEN BURIED, TOO!

WHAAH! ALL THE PRESENTS, FOOD, DECORATIONS...

CRUSHED! WIPED OUT!

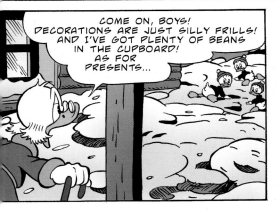

COME ON, BOYS! DECORATIONS ARE JUST SILLY FRILLS! AND I'VE GOT PLENTY OF BEANS IN THE CUPBOARD! AS FOR PRESENTS...

MY FIRST DIME IS SAFE! *THAT'S* THE BEST GIFT WE COULD GET!

UNCLE SCROOGE! YOU OUGHT TO BE ASHAMED OF YOURSELF!

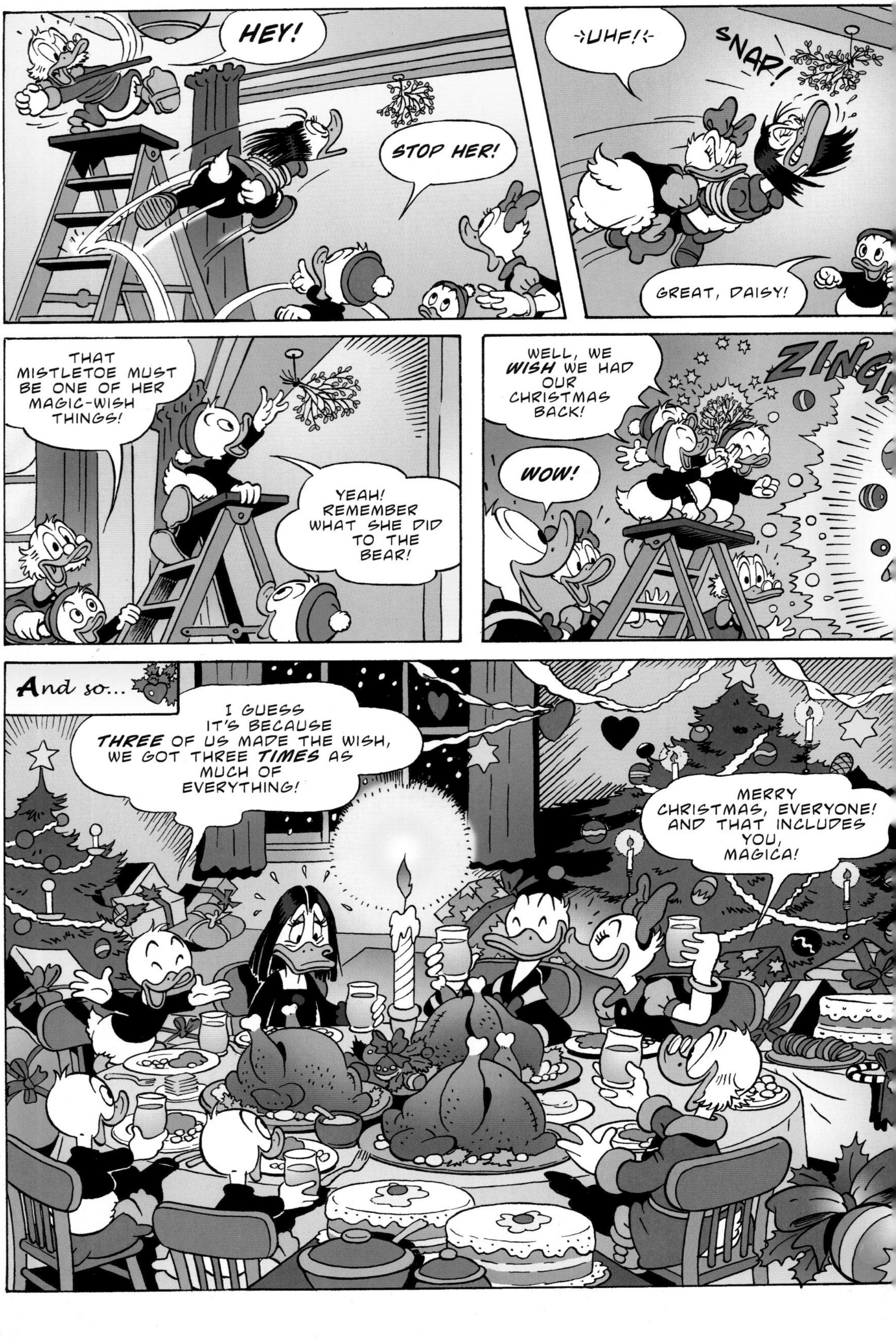
HEY!
STOP HER!
-UHF!-
SNAP!
GREAT, DAISY!
THAT MISTLETOE MUST BE ONE OF HER MAGIC-WISH THINGS!
YEAH! REMEMBER WHAT SHE DID TO THE BEAR!
WELL, WE WISH WE HAD OUR CHRISTMAS BACK!
WOW!
ZING!
And so...
I GUESS IT'S BECAUSE THREE OF US MADE THE WISH, WE GOT THREE TIMES AS MUCH OF EVERYTHING!
MERRY CHRISTMAS, EVERYONE! AND THAT INCLUDES YOU, MAGICA!